The Poetry Weaver:

The Song I Came To Sing

Diane Lipton Gollub

New York

Publishing Consultant: Brandy Lane
Cover Background: SueAnn Summers
Cover Art: Diane Lipton Gollub
Foreword: Hayley Meredith Gollub

Published in the United States of America by:
Diane Lipton Gollub
Ingram Premium Softcover ISBN: 979-8-9913735-1-7

Library of Congress Control Number: 2024912824

Publishing Consultant:
Formatting, supporting edits,
photo color edits, and layout design.
Brandy Lane of Where Beautiful Inks LLC.

Author's Portrait by: East 27 Creative
All other decorative art throughout this book is
licensed through Canva and Canva Pro memberships.

Dedication

For my late husband, Monte Jonathan Gollub
and my children,
Hayley Meredith Gollub and Ross Brandon Gollub.

Mixed Media

Author's Note

This collection contains my perceptions and reflections upon the fleeting facets of life: childhood, love, marriage, parenthood, love lost, widowhood, grief, societal and environmental shifts. Included as well, are pieces of art which I've done at various stages of my life: pencil drawings, etchings, pastels, aquatints, watercolors, photography, and mixed media.

I am a Baby Boomer, a daughter, an artist, an attorney, a mother, an American citizen, and an active philanthropist. Some aspects of me are ephemeral; some endure, becoming the lens through which I experience life.

There are those memories that forever endure, like indelible slices of childhood. The levels of emotion within all relationships formed, the fortune found in soulmate love, the unimaginable squelching of happiness and sudden submersion into all-consuming grief upon the unexpected loss of my husband of twenty-five years.

It is through these poems that I have exorcized the sorrow felt so deeply, enabling me to again find the light.

I have witnessed such drastic changes in America within my decades of living, Born into a country in civil unrest, my generation believed in our ability to make a positive difference. We had promise and hope.

Now, I'm witnessing the retraction of freedoms, the intolerance of too many who have been empowered to alter the course of our nation, pivoting dangerously away from its intended gift of freedom.

My concern for the environment is portrayed, as we all bear witness, its degradation unraveling ever more rapidly.

My work as an Assistant District Attorney in New York led me to realize the magnitude of the need for attention that must be given to educating our children, indeed all men and women, about the varying forms of abuse; the appropriate legal means of intervention, ever so critical to relate. My experience visiting high schools, outlining child abuse law, impacted me greatly.

My hope is that, through the poetry conveyed, others may find promise in the potential for light to be found in life. The importance of living in each moment, soaking in happiness whilst it is occurring. If immersed within the depth of sorrow, time, can perhaps, ease its pain. It is within each of us to shift our perspective to again find promise.

—Diane

Pencil on sketch paper

Special Thanks

The journey back from the most profound grief can be seemingly endless. It is an individualized experience from which some never quite recover.

I am blessed with children who have been by my side during the most harrowing of tragedies. Almost twenty years ago, they lost their father, and I, my husband, far too soon.

Once widowed, I became consumed within the opaque darkness of the sorrow that defines heartache. Then, some time later, I discovered the Instagram poetry community—it was there that I began writing poetry, and revisiting my love of writing, something I had done throughout my college years. I entered a form of catharsis through penning my pain.

The online poetry community immediately embraced this Baby Boomer. International writers began reading my work in live streams, and I received sensitive feedback from this incredibly loving and nurturing group of artists.

Specifically, I wish to thank Angela Psalm for her unwavering love and support from Australia; Philip Carmen, for continuously extending his love and support from England, sharing the photo taken by him at The Lost Gardens of Heligan, which inspired the writing of "Moss Woman"; Steve Buttigieg, for sharing his sagacious counsel from Belgium; Tommy Disarro, for advising me so encouragingly and prudently from Florida; SueAnn Summers, an artist, and poet who took the time to nurture me as I approached this venture, providing the green fresco background for my cover; and all those who have become beloved to me through the online poetry community.

It would not have been possible to have laid out my wealth of words without the unending care and guidance from Brandy Lane. Her creativity and patience were tested, making changes over and over, line by line until I was satisfied. Brandy adjusted every inappropriate space, switched to the specific fonts which I chose, and framed my individual pieces of art and photos contained herein, truly becoming one with my vision.

Special love and thanks to beloved Julie Ann Keleher for believing in me beyond measure, endlessly reading through my work along with me, forging my connection with Brandy and inspiring me to create this book, my first.

—Diane

Foreword

At her core, Diane is an artist. She always has been. She depicts reality, and not just the pretty. She feels deeply and paints with words in profound ways. Diane's exceptional use of written expression is fundamental to who she is as a person; to her, the process of creation and emotional release is equally important to the poetic outcomes penned on pages. Her work is art in its most authentic form, for Diane is a poetry weaver whose words are authentically born straight from her sensitive soul. In THE SONG I CAME TO SING, they now become your tapestry.

Herein, Diane writes about the immense power of a word and suggests we use language wisely, to impart kindness. As a mother, Diane certainly does just that.

And I should know, as I'm Diane's daughter.

Adorned with stickers and drafted on cheerful stationery, handwritten letters were lovingly mailed to my sleepaway camp so I did not miss an ounce of her summer adventures while embarking on those of my own. She crafted thoughtful poems for my brother brimming with empathy for the boyhood challenge of the moment. There were perfectly composed (and promptly issued) thank-you notes for even the smallest gestures of kindness bestowed upon our family. I found caring notes in my lunchbox on school days, and when I was older, tucked away in my suitcase on trips.

My mom is the person who speaks up – with intelligence and grace – when everyone else remains silent. She's the stylish, friendly face that strangers approach in the department store to ask for fashion advice. She's the legal brain that people in distress call for wise counsel. She's the pianist whose musical notes permeate the house as intensely as the scent of her delectable home-cooking. She's the mother who is so fun and beloved that even her children's friends ask her to hang out. Despite an irreplaceable space in her heart from the devastating loss of my father, she's the widow who carries on, for she is an independent woman of substance.

Simply stated, she's a multi-hyphenate. There's no singular word to describe Diane, and there's no simple box in which she can be contained. My mom has character, integrity, and a generous spirit. Always affording an unconventional outlook that makes you think twice, she's just enormously *interesting* – even her striking turquoise eyes contain a splash of hazel mixed in for good measure! To have her in your life is to be one of the lucky ones. And to never *(ever)* be bored.

In THE SONG I CAME TO SING, audiences will get a significant dose of my brilliant mom, her life experiences, her passions, her observations, her beliefs, and the inner workings of her truly mesmerizing mind. Themes include Life & Love, Grief, Nature & Earth, The Facets of a Nation, Inhumane Humanity, and Wisdom & Hope. All is authentically her, and all is passionately delivered directly from the heart, like everything she gives to this world.

You'll find she claims the song she came to sing remains unsung, but after reading her debut poetry collection, I believe we'll *all* question if that's in fact true...

Because she's always been singing, and she's an artist who always will: "I will remain on fire," Diane fiercely pens. Her music is the most important, influential soundtrack of my life. And now it's your turn to soak in the epic poetry.

Happy Reading!

With Love,

—*Hayley Meredith Gollub*

Table of Contents

The Song I Came To Sing 2

LIFE & LOVE

Through The Love Of Poetry 6

A Lesson In Grace 7

Sticks And Stones 8

Trepidation 10

The Silent Storm Chaser 11

Indigo Haze 12

The Features Of Fate 14

I Will Remain On Fire 15

In The Bleeding Moonlight 16

Solitude 18

Loving You Was Hard 20

If I Could Forget Yesterday 22

Freckled Shoulders 23

Gratitude 24

Beloved Son 26

Ode To My Daughter 28

Time Forever Fleeting 30

Shredded Journals 32

Life Lessons Learned 34

My Sharp Edges 36

Let The Core Breathe 37

LIFE & LOVE

Purpose Stems From Passion 38

Irresistible, Insatiable Ink 40

Wealth Of Wrinkles 41

Making My Heart Whole 42

Give Me Back 43

Closure 44

A Day In The Life Of A Poet 46

GRIEF

A Perfect Storm Gathered Cosmic Clusters Of Stars 50

I Let Go Of Myself 52

Poem To My Younger Self 54

Why Would I Be Infatuated With You? 56

Deep In My Heart 58

Tomorrow Is Not Promised 60

The Warmth Of His Smile 62

Lost In The Fog Of Tomorrow 64

Cascade Of Pain Ruptured Through My Veins 66

Deep And Dangerous Like The Sea 68

The Realm Where Dreams Roam Free 70

The Hands That Let Me Go 71

You Sailed Away From Our Empty Nest 72

The Letters I Wrote 74

GRIEF

A Longing That Danced Like A Moth To A Flame 76

Fractured Reflections 78

Alone I Must Weep 79

True Loss 80

Ink And Shadows 82

The Power And Pull Of Two Hearts That Are Full 83

Closing Time 84

I Wish I Could Hear Voices 86

NATURE & EARTH

Beautiful Madness 90

The Spark Of Brilliance 91

Ode To The Earth 92

I Immerse Myself Beneath Calm Waters 94

We Are The Daisies 96

The Paradox Of Daffodils 98

Destiny Dreamed 99

Aries Reborn 100

Dreaming Of Evergreens 102

Sea Breeze Wrapped In Sorrow 104

Utopian Garden 106

Moss Woman 107

All That Remains 108

Grow With The Wildflowers 110

NATURE & EARTH

Bleeding Willow 112

Hold My Hand A Little Longer 114

Springtime's Floral Breath 116

Rippling River 118

An Unperturbed Lake 119

Beloved of Autumn 120

Blue Ice 122

Footprints On Glaciers 123

Sitting In The Moon 124

Stardust Parade 126

Befallen Dusk 127

The Monarch Butterfly 128

THE FACETS OF A NATION

Early Times Of Sweet Youth 130

Back When I Believed..132

Oh, To Be The Thunder.....................................134

When Tears Fall Like Cosmic Dust 136

The Tightrope Walker 137

Love Is The Religion...138

Lifeblood...139

RBG..140

Women Give Life, Demand Freedom! 142

THE FACETS OF A NATION

The Puppet Master 144

It's True What They Say 145

The Un-Creator 146

Open Air Prison..148

Life Goes On 149

"Six Year Old Left To Play With A Smith & Wesson".......150

Mental Health Awareness..152

Crucified Hope In Turquoise Waters 154

The Essence Of A Bully 156

Intervention 158

Resurrection Of America 159

No Grades For Kindness 160

Angels And Demons..162

Freedom Stripped Away..164

INHUMANE HUMANITY

Combustible..168

A Fragile Notion 170

If I Could Save The World 171

Tonight, The Moon Saw Me Cry.................................172

Nightmares 174

The Gardens Of Your Own Reality............................175

INHUMANE HUMANITY

Humanity, On The Verge Of Extinction......................176

Echoing In Silence 177

Unravel With The Wind To Be Free..........................178

Synthetic Embrace 179

Abuse...180

No One Hears Her Screams....................................182

Vengeance Is Mine...184

If Love Could Kill 186

You Can't Take It Back 188

Bohemian Rhapsody..190

Weirdo...192

Dachau 194

Seeds Of Doubt 197

Seasons Of The Soul..198

Prayers For Peace Never Virtually Vanish 200

From Whence Stems Hatred Harbored?.......................201

My Family Tree..202

Pull Me Past The Pain 204

Their Pernicious Journey 205

Empathetic Distress 206

Peace Is A Privilege For Minds Like Us 208

WISDOM & HOPE

The Shared Pen 210

Love Is Not An Illusion 211

The Poetry Weaver...212

Sands Of Time 213

Savor The Taste Of Humbleness.............................214

The Soloist 216

Kudos To "Good Will Hunting" 218

Release Me...220

What Sound Is Heard At The End of Time?.................222

Appreciation Gained Through Thoughtfulness.............223

Embrace The Glorious Mess That Is You 224

Petals Of Change 226

This Moment In Time...228

Fractured Promises 229

Symphony Of Sorrow...230

Art's Eternal Embrace 232

How You Lose Her 234

When A Dream Is Born In You..............................235

The Scent Of Paper 236

Let Go Of Fears 238

How Much Can One Heart Hold? 240

Caged In Your Regrets 241

WISDOM & HOPE

One Hug Turns Every Tear Into Radiant Rays...............242

Dare To Care 243

Pinpoints..244

I Am Woman..246

Fleeting Facets...247

May It Be Rainbows That You See............................248

Fearlessly Allow Your Facets To Shine 250

Hope For A Brighter Tomorrow 252

Those Wonders Unveiled In Spring...........................254

And If I Were To Die Today....................................256

The Poetry Weaver:

The Song I Came To Sing

Diane Lipton Gollub

The Song I Came To Sing

The story is told
that Mom jumped up and down,
and out came Diane,
smiles all around!

Born with a curiosity
typical of a cat,
creating endless adventures
at the drop of a hat.

Though I adored frolicking,
playing with friends,
my imagination was my favorite
companion in the end.

Memorizing every musical,
acting out every scene,
lost in a world of artistry,
is where I felt most serene.

Contemporaneous with this,
compassion always in my eyes,
well aware so many
were not as fortunate as I.

Diane Lipton Gollub

Pastel

Bringing home stray pets,
helping another soul who seemed spent,
'twas the best gift I could give
wherever I went.

Helping those who were hungry,
fighting for social change,
belief that wrongs could be righted
if perspectives were rearranged.

In an ever-evolving life,
I have always refused to look away,
for the song I came to sing
remains unsung to this day.

Diane Lipton Gollub

Life & Love

Through The Love Of Poetry

Once upon a poem, there comes a time
when ink to paper yields bountiful lines of rhyme.
Whatever chaos might exist in my head,
I attempt to iron it out through words written or said.

Humanity, perpetually at odds with each other,
irrational hatred, uncontained.
Former friends or family suddenly abhor
those they had believed to be their sisters or brothers—
now, enemies they remain.

Nature rightfully unleashing her wrath—
her fury for being abused.
Anxiety compounding, as too much tragedy abounds;
a world is left confused.

As an artist, I have learned,
this disquiet can be redirected
into creativity—attempting to keep
my own heart protected.

Discontent is the fuel I now use.

Magically brilliant solutions,
I am not arrogant enough to offer,
but through the love of poetry—life lessons learned,
perhaps rays of hope are what I can proffer.

A Lesson In Grace

School provided a stage upon which I could shine,
good grades came easily, a quick study was I.
I could readily ascertain, practically since birth,
that in which others found their worth.

The ability to adapt and attune to a task—
regurgitate correct answers to all questions asked.
Upon leaving one venue to arrive at another
I pretended I was placed on a mission, undercover.

An observer of life is what I became,
quite the variety of cliques knew my name.
It became clear that many were not a part of the fun,
perhaps shy, some sad, they seemed to hang out with no one.

Nothing specific really set them apart,
but I could sense the heaviness that was in their hearts.
Slowly reaching out to them once in a while,
sensitively attempting to get them to smile.

The greatest lesson I learned which brought my life grace,
was extending kindness, so simple, can bring light to a face.

Sticks And Stones

What makes one culture
different from another?
How is a child influenced
by their father or mother?

How is the art
of poetry defined?
What gives it the power
to affect one's state of mind?

Creating perceptions,
evoking emotion,
strong enough to shift
notion to notion.

As children, we are taught not to flinch—
not to seem too affected,
when this weapon is unleashed
upon those unprotected.

So powerful,
able to crush a soul to the core,
cause depression—
make someone question their worth anymore.

This great influencer
can be either read or heard,
what this describes
is the immense power of a WORD.

Words can shape our personalities,
can alter beliefs,
when written or spoken kindly,
they can give one relief.

Encouragement is felt
when positively used,
but they also possess the strength to shatter,
to make one feel abused.

A sense of self readily can be formed,
by words heard or read.
Be mindful of the power
to impart kindness instead.

Trepidation

Can't find my footing,
facing the vastness of the sea,
sand washing away
as each new tide cascades beneath me.
Feeling my chest tighten,
panic begins to take hold,
so much uncertainty,
the next wave unfolds.
Afraid to move forward,
nothing of substance to hold,
with extreme trepidation,
I force myself to feel bold.
I begin to envision
a structure, secure, enveloping me,
breathe in, breathe out,
repeat,
calming my nerves,
courage found within positivity,
I am now free to emerge.

The Silent Storm Chaser

In fierce, fiery, fueled fashion,
there was little that fazed her,
lethal as a force of nature,
dubbed,
The Silent Storm Chaser.
Vigilantly scanning the globe
to end another's plight,
methodically, expeditiously
altering wrongs,
making them right.

Indigo Haze

Whilst a child, convinced I was dropped
into a family not my own—
always contemplative, deemed overly sensitive,
critiques which cut to the bone.

Befuddled by what seemed
to be arbitrary parameters set,
frustrated when limited by others
who required their own expectations to be met.

Immersing myself passionately
into each task undertaken,
perplexed when others dismissed my positivity
as utterly mistaken.

'Twas early when I realized
the cosmos is grand,
though mere specks of dust, no doubt
we were intentionally placed on this land.

Innate was a belief
that intolerance was untoward,
a wall erected by those
who lacked the inner conviction to look forward.

Wars initiated by those
who remained too blind to see,
that dichotomy could coexist
amidst amicable harmony.

Diane Lipton Gollub

Acid etching

It is within an indigo haze I choose to reside,
forever hopeful that humanity
shall learn to live side by side,
partaking in respect for each other—
whilst inspiring pride.

The Features Of Fate

The inception of romance,
forever encapsulated
within magnificent memories made—
the profound purity and glorious freshness
that lies in the beginning;
both given the chance
to be on equal footing,
no one yet losing or winning.

When sensations consume completely,
unveiling within a magical mystery—
the dynamic dance of desire done,
moving towards an aspired destiny.

Careful to include sufficient constructs
of those subtle signs of sensuality,
reeling within the heat of each other—
passion precisely peaked and played,
discordance yet unrecognized.

But, beware,
there is no one not subject to
the features of fate—
what has already been written
in the sun, moon and stars.

Prisoners we are of the laws of probability,
that has brought each person
to where they now are.

Diane Lipton Gollub

I Will Remain On Fire

Born an Aries, the moon and stars
willed me great passion,
every task undertaken by me,
done with concerted action.

Striving to live with honor,
integrity, devotion,
having personally experienced
the conflagration of disparate emotions.

Judiciously assessing
prudent solutions to sever strife,
whether personal to me,
or crippling the quality of another's life.

As evil prevails when good people do nothing
to prevent its perpetuation,
throughout my years I've fiercely advocated,
attempting to improve another's situation.

However, societal shifts
have eradicated all notions of hope—it's soured,
an electorate has neglected due diligence
in selecting whom they've empowered.

Though the magnitude required to now survive
has become monumental,
I will remain on fire in firm opposition
to that which is inevitably detrimental.

In The Bleeding Moonlight

In the bleeding moonlight,
my psyche has rendered me inert, energy wanes,
a spirit that always bursts with positivity
no longer remains.

How much sorrow
can one heart hold?
What endurance when assaulted
with tragedies so cold?

In tune with its rhythm,
the core of our being,
the rush of blood surging forth continuously
while we are breathing—
its choreographed dance
with the brain, so unique,
one readily affecting the other
within an aura of mystique.

But, then, is heartbreak
actually perceived in the brain?
Causing a depth of despair
that can drive one insane?

Have had my fill of debilitating emotions,
so enervating,
once again yearn to pursue tangible risks
that are worth taking.

With courage anew, I hold on to the moon,
an eternal source of inspiration,
leaning into the quest to unveil joy again
through renewed contemplation.

Solitude

Been alive
long enough to see,
societal shifts
erratically changing before me.

Whilst young,
raised in a society that appreciated respect,
certainly learned early
that losing is part of the life that we get.

Observed that dignity within
was what steered us each to paths that were true,
disappointment—part of lessons learned,
essential, to be valued.

Each generation
compelled to stand in judgment of those before,
a rite of passage
prior to entering adulthood's door.

But family was essential,
sharing both joys and sorrows,
crucial support systems
with uncertain tomorrows.

Guidance of elders, given when requested,
the perspective of those who have lived life, been tested,
not always accepted when dispensed and suggested,
served to make one's kin a sacred haven of hope.

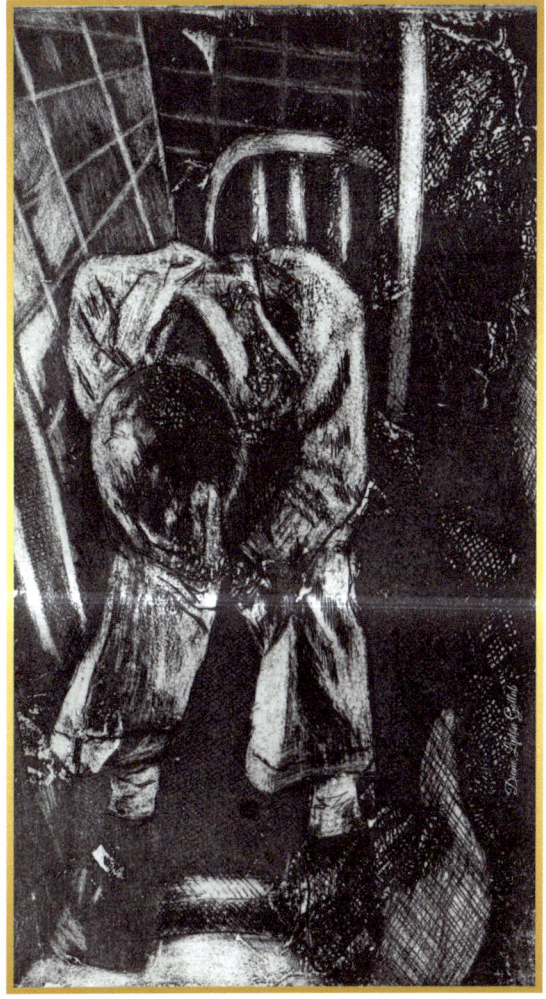

Acid etching

However today,
families have moved
so far away,
generations
compartmentalized,
within separate
residences,
they stay.

Now feeling I've lived
significantly
past my prime,
a relic left over
from a forgotten time.

I walk alone through
what will remain
of my years,
my heart heavy—
within solitude,
I shed my tears.

Loving You Was Hard

From the perspective of one born
with a sensitive, emotional disposition;
loving you was hard,
in that, you maintained a dispassionate position.

Seemingly not attuned to the concept of emotional intelligence,
no inkling, indeed,
of the consequence of your apparent indifference
to your children's individual needs.

Having attained extraordinary success in your career,
this brilliance took its toll,
you chose a perspective, indeed t'was selective,
not investing energy into that which you deemed
outside your control.

Loving you was hard,
but I was forever malleable,
accommodating your limitations,
I remained flexible,
for Dad, to me,
you remained on a pedestal.

Whilst a young child,
I'd sit quietly by your side,
no need for attention—
a mountain of complex legal contracts had to be rewritten
prior to receiving your affirmation.

But when I went through the greatest loss in my life,
all too swiftly spun out of control,
you could not fathom
that my soul now had a hole.

Then came the time when your life fell apart,
you learned the true meaning of a broken heart—
my beloved mother, your devoted wife,
all too suddenly lost her life.
Suddenly you came to comprehend,
the magnitude of all-consuming pain, with no end.

Loving you was hard, Dad.

Always, your adoring daughter.

If I Could Forget Yesterday

If I forgot my yesterdays,
I would have no place in my universe—
for layers upon layers of experiences
have resulted in my essence today,
to further change in the morrow.
Life is a continuous journey,
its content comprised of those roads traveled.

The stars did determine my soulmate,
then gifted us progeny, each unique,
what an immense chasm would penetrate my being
if I were to have ever forgotten them today.

Mindful that beauty can be found
in surfing the crests of waves,
contrasted with the pain experienced
upon crashing into troughs—
only to then rise again.

If I could forget yesterday,
for certain—
I would have no means to measure pleasure.

Freckled Shoulders

It's been so many years since your eyes last closed,
serenely laying in a hospital bed, as if you'd been posed.
I always took for granted that you would be near,
foolishly quarreling over nonsense while you were here.

The most titanic soul to ever walk planet Earth,
graciously giving of yourself to help others find worth.
Forever a force of nature,
you continued to support and make sure
I could achieve any heights to which I tried to soar.

Family first was how you demonstrated priorities,
always there—perhaps crossword puzzles in hand,
or outside, on your knees,
cutting Dad's blooms or weeding under the trees.

My childhood house, always a welcome place to be,
how vacant it suddenly became without you there next to me.
A brilliant woman of pure integrity always spoke your mind,
I truly cannot recall you once saying anything unkind.

With summer now before me, in tears, recalling years of imagery,
it's your lovely face, Mom, your freckled shoulders—
that I still vividly see.

Gratitude

Motherhood, a mystery, so baffling to me,
never held a baby, now adding to our family tree.

Always one to give one hundred fifty percent,
I attempted to unravel—
those volumes of information written
in countless books of pure psycho babble.

Ever the academic, devouring instruction,
literally outlining each developmental stage,
preoccupied with whether the behavior of my children
coincided with the content of each page.

This new priority caused such a significant shift,
my days turning upside down;
one child followed the Golden Rule,
the other—forever a cute clown.

So unfamiliar, that such great effort could be expended
with no immediate recognizable return,
impossible to yet know what, if anything,
my children will learn.

Cycles of their lives forever evolving,
the uncertainty of its outcome, so strange,
before me I am watching as my children's growth
continues to rearrange.

Nowadays I spend time reminiscing,
examining the wealth of pictures that fill my rooms;
with gratitude I realize, that my greatest gift has been bearing witness
as my daughter and son continue to bloom.

Photograph by DLG

Beloved Son

Beloved son,
almost twenty years since I passed,
now, unable to speak with you
in a language that will last.

Forever in my heart,
my thoughts of you continue, unending,
if there only existed a means to package them
into something tangible—then sending.

For you were my shadow, my buddy,
your energy mirrored mine,
like an Energizer battery,
you needed so little sleep to be able to shine.

Fishing with me while still a small dude—
only three,
we hauled in bluefish off Great Point, Nantucket,
excitedly shrieking with glee!

Yes, I had to help you a little,
but you took to it right away,
taught you the art of fileting fish,
our dinners—enjoyed with our catch of the day!

Proceeding to become a yachtsman
at the age of eight,
an adult boating license earned—
you, my First Mate!

Photograph by DLG

When setting your mind to something,
there is nothing you cannot learn.

Please know, my child,
in my soul we still sit, fishing on a pier,
forever a part of each other,
you are never without me, my dear.

Ode To My Daughter

Having grown into a woman
of significant substance and depth,
forever endowed with the unique ability
to take away my breath.

Decades ago, upon learning
you were housed within me, so serene,
four months had already passed, unknowingly,
you, the essence of tranquility, a dream.

Endured those early months
filled with prosecutorial trials I conducted,
held steadfast within me
during equestrian jumps I constructed.

Emerging during a blizzard, four weeks early
to our surprise and delight,
forever a ray of sunshine, a bounty in our lives.

A continuing source of pride,
"Daddy's Sweetheart", until the day he died.

Soaring above hardships,
through sorrows which emerged, unexpected,
continuously striving to achieve mastery
in all you attempted.

So humbly,
well earned respect enjoyed
from those with whom you have worked
throughout your years.
Undertaking complex negotiations and projects,
the recipient of respect amongst your peers.

My beloved daughter, it is with immense pride
that I proclaim you to be my closest confidante,
indeed in possession of all attributes
any mother could want.

Time Forever Fleeting

If I only knew when young
that time was forever fleeting,
I would have soaked in every moment,
appreciating each to the max.
One's world is so small in childhood,
negotiating all stimuli within it;
for one so young,
a daunting task.

Children seeing, hearing, feeling their surroundings,
absorbing relationships observed,
becoming the perspectives they emulate,
at every turn—
for children, truly live what they learn.
With sensitivity they ingest
those varying components of
joy,
suffering,
tolerance,
hostility,
hopefully—goodness.

The consequence either warms their hearts,
or causes anxiety—undue stress.
Should evil arrive in their paradise,
balance achieved,
can forever shift.

If only I knew then, whilst a child,
time would be forever fleeting
throughout my life.

Photograph by Harvey Lee Lipton

Shredded Journals

Worlds become mine,
a new foray found, entering any author's mind
whilst immersed in literary creations,
their imaginations served to stir my sensations.

Stream of consciousness through prose penned,
liberated my artistic soul,
permission granted to write freely,
herein release all semblance of control.

My journals became a staple
of each and every day,
they became the friends who heard
what I needed to say.

As life presented challenges
consequential decisions to be made,
my journals became the playground
in which my thoughts could freely play.

Diane Lipton Gollub

Never once did I reread them,
the process, itself, was the key
to unlock each puzzle,
through which to resolve each mystery.

Recalling with specificity
upon becoming engaged,
choosing to meld my life with another—
the thrill of knowing new roads were to be paved.

Intentionally shredding my journals,
those private roads already traveled,
to begin anew, with my soulmate by my side,
complexities to come, would together, be unraveled.

Life Lessons Learned

Life lessons learned
through wisdom gained,
the cure for hearts broken depends greatly
on the cause of the pain.

Shattering, pinpoint pricks of agony,
searing, crippling,
existence, now precarious,
sinking down,
down,
down,
all semblance of my former reality,
instantaneously dissolved—
entering the void of heartbreak
from the sudden death of my mate.

This, a rarity.

Far more frequently experienced,
easier to withstand,
is learning the cure,
when those now mistaken for friends
cause sorrow through absentia, planned.
The jarring stabs suffered,
when abandoned by those I believed to be cherished,
deciding to now leave me at the worst time of my life,
from this, I became extinguished.

Left alone
to raise my children on my own,
broken,
bleeding in blue,
no clarity within view.

Lessons learned, the key to this cure,
examine the degree of respect held
for the one who caused the pain so endured—
who, when tragedy blasted me out of my zone,
walked away from me when my life was not fun,
left me alone in my marital home.

Abandoning me—
one who had always chosen
to be there when I should,
continuously did what needed doing—
whatever I could,
leaving me now, feeling so raw,
misunderstood.

The power to continue to hurt my heart
shall heretofore not be granted—
this they will not get.
For I shall not waste a moment on those
who turned their backs—
lacked regret for leaving.

My time, too precious,
life continues,
forever fleeting.

My Sharp Edges

Born with the sun in Aries,
so I am, through and through,
blessed with a heart that contains endless passion,
once trusted within my persona,
I am entirely devoted to you.

I will lead with courage,
bravely undertaking what few risk to do;
creatively weaving a plan of attack,
negotiating obstacles as they appear—
my dedication remains true.

But beware not to cross my loving heart,
for I am a fire sign, which will readily ignite.

My sharp edges will begin to cut to the quick,
slicing...
You'll then be
scorched
out of
sight.

Let The Core Breathe

That's how quickly it happens.
Surroundings start spinning,
my heart begins racing,
a cold sweat descending,
as I am circuitously pacing,
my body goes numb
while I shake to the bone,
all numbers start to blur
when I look at my phone.
Pulsating pounding pressure
pressing on my chest,
cannot focus at all,
as my brain will not rest,
summoning forth the will
to grind things to a halt...
begin chanting silently,
panic attacks—not my fault.
Recalling the psycho babble
uttered repeatedly to me,
by people with degrees in psychiatry.
Don't fight this progression,
have a seat, let it be—
let the core breathe in and out,
slowly release.
This, too, shall pass,
no doubt, within a few minutes,
I'll be eased.

Purpose Stems From Passion

How meticulously spiders craft
the webs that they weave
creating artistry through
those graphic patterns they leave.

Views from my home,
now obstructed, streaks on the glass,
for no one has bothered to clean
in a year and a half.

Books, brochures, magazines
lined up within piles,
no interest in concentrating
on them for awhile.

Lawn overgrown,
once pristine landscaping,
all now askew,
no longer the domicile that people once knew.

Choosing not to be dismantled
by all listed above,
electing instead to focus
on what now can bring love.

Stroking the keys of my piano
with renewed insight,
strumming songs on my guitar,
humming melodies created within songs I might write,
creating fine art
while viewing all in plain sight.

Lifting a pen to scribe
new poetry, prose,
unique expressions emerge
of the *me* no one knows.

Emanating from within
springs new-found inspiration.
For nothing can diminish
quality to be found
in those heartfelt results
of purpose
stemming
from passion.

Irresistible, Insatiable Ink

Within a stream of consciousness,
eternal, never-ending,
flows the content of my pondering,
poetry pending.
Birthed onto paper,
unique representations
resulting from irresistible insatiable ink—
my creations.

That magical moment,
crystallizing cascading words,
attempting to capture inner sensations.
But in one moment's time,
perceptions change,
suddenly springs a new one, divine!

Yielding a rhythmic refrain
pouring out of my brain,
indeed the life of a poet
can drive one insane!
Such is the craving,
which eternally remains—
which a writer possesses whilst inking,
a world altered when blinking,
a curative method of sorting through chaos contained.

Wealth Of Wrinkles

Awaken to the beauty to be found,
virtually traced,
those etched emotions formed
from the wealth of wrinkles
on one's face—
these lines, the true markers that remain,
from a life lived with grace.

Our society now possessed—
obsessed with eradicating the history of our years,
Botox-revered,
as all remain so steeped in fear
of revealing the souvenirs
of surprise, joy, laughter, and tears.

The inexplicably irrational need that society feeds
of hiding those memories
of a life fully lived—absurd indeed.
A literal air-brushing of purported imperfections
reduces individuality to a standard—approved.
I find it a shock to again meet someone known in my youth—
for I no longer see the friend I once knew.

Missing now are those pieces of truth
which, indeed, make us each unique.
It is frightening to not view as complete,
old friends whose shared history
contains the comfort I seek.

Making My Heart Whole

An exorcism begins
during the process of throwing the clay,
smashing it again and again,
releasing those air bubbles in the way.

Staring at this shapeless mound
that now lay before me,
envisioning what to subtract from its surface,
to extract what I see.

Methodically rotating its surface,
to not neglect any angle,
mindful to deftly use my tools—
not to mangle.

Experience teaches when it's time that day to walk away,
cover with moist cloths, wrap intact,
for when viewing it in the morrow,
I might sense what it lacks.

When finally concluding,
it is now finished, complete,
that feeling of giving birth fills my soul,
for its creation is unique.

Diane Lipton Gollub

Give Me Back

Give me back those decades of time
already passed,
with innocent ignorance,
no comprehension that nothing lasts.

Wasted years wished away,
wantonly wanting,
an endless quest for tangible meaning to make itself known,
remaining forlorn, forever daunting.

Days turn into weeks,
weeks into years,
foolishly believing there exists forever,
to again sink my teeth
into new endeavors.

But the seesaw has tilted,
once was up, now I'm down,
nearer to the end of forever,
the scope of missed opportunities compounds.

Now, with wisdom gained,
cognizant to not waste a day,
Behold,
the increased volume
of time ticking away.

Closure

When you've chosen to live your whole life,
lifting spirits of others suffering strife,
giving all that you could,
breaking down walls when you should,
suddenly,
silence can cut like a knife.

Spending countless hours, days and years—
soothing those troubled,
while drying their tears.
Patiently sorting through their cries
sourced from their fears—
holding hands of fragile souls,
always loved so dear.

That quiet, so sudden,
no phones now ring in my home,
the hollow impact
of knowing I'm truly alone.

When most of the family you had from the start,
have chosen to forget
that you gave them your heart,
hosted parties galore,
celebrating them and more,
facing the harsh reality—
you've grown apart.

After years of speculation,
wondering why,
reaching the conclusion
they've let my value slip by;
it's time to move on,
accept they are gone.
Closure.

A Day In The Life Of A Poet

An artist possessing a mind that does not rest,
continuously consuming perceptions of life—
at its worst, at its best.

Devastated by unending disasters
which befall victims in the world,
creativity enables me to liberate my spirit, unfurled.

Always moved by the magnificence of music,
I feel it touch my heart;
then motivated to play the ebonies and ivories
as the day becomes dark.

Dissecting landscapes, still-lifes,
people as they appear in my view—
breaking them into their particular components
of texture and hue,
then rendering them with pastels
into a version so true.

During litigation, persuasively formulating legal arguments—
a creative endeavor,
when opposing sentiments yield consternation,
who shall emerge—deemed more clever?

But, a day in the life of a poet would not be complete,
without penning the flow of verbiage
soaring through my mind, to a beat;
a form of catharsis,
each uniquely our own,
while working to convey the content of a poem.

Pastel

Portable therapy
free to be utilized wherever I roam,
a virtual stream of consciousness
pouring out of my soul;
such that after penning a piece,
if perchance, I am pleased,
I am appeased,
that my soul indeed has found release.

GRIEF

A PERFECT STORM GATHERED COSMIC CLUSTERS OF STARS

Vacant years violated
with virtual memories, past,
the promise of forever,
was one I was not able to make last.

Decades ago, yielding entry,
you touched my heart and soul,
both foolishly unaware—in youth, so ignorant,
that eternity was well beyond our control.

Perpetual anguish persists,
continuously missing you so,
for we had become one,
our lives together, not done,
I still cannot let you go.

I remain struggling—
stuck at an impasse.

A mere shell of you was what we buried,
those remains, so vividly etched.
The moment you left,
when your body could no longer stir—
this, for certain, was not who you were.

All these years since,
I maintain the strain—
finding it impossible to
connect with you once again—
missing my soulmate, lover,
husband, best friend.

Now a perfect storm has gathered
within a cosmic cluster of stars,
perchance promise shall permit
entry into the mist—
granting me access
to where you now exist.

I LET GO OF MYSELF

Once upon a time,
I believed myself blessed,
when life handed me lemons,
my lemonade was the best.

My calendar marked every approaching event,
my intent that for those I cared—
flowers, cards, gifts were dispensed.
However, when the balance
does unexpectedly shift,
I discovered that the tightrope
I had walked when blessed,
was precarious, swaying, wavering,
when put to the test.

How shocking becomes the realization
once calamity descends unexpectedly,
the true substance of what constituted
those friendships formed—
becomes an eye-opening reality.
Quickly learning of empathy's scarcity,
its absence quite profound,
once one's world is consumed by emotional distress,
no one chooses to remain around.

For those whose lives have remained intact,
without fault, clueless to sorrow so deep—
their offers to dance, dine, and frolic,
became incomprehensible to me.

Left alone within smothering solitude,
I could not help but compare,
others who had faced similar loss,
given time, they found new loves to share.

But everyone has an experience that is unique.
I found myself sinking into darkness so bleak.
The few friends who remained,
requested I let go of the pain,
but I had already sunken so deep.

I was immersed within guilt that did not abate,
something so dark to which they could not relate,
for failing to cure my lifelong mate.

I instead chose to let go of myself for so long,
finding no place where I could truly belong.

POEM TO MY YOUNGER SELF

I write this poem to my younger self,
countless photos, of which rest on my shelves—
in eyes so young I see the light,
belief that endless possibilities are in sight.

I try, I fail, then try again,
with an inner conviction that I was a strong woman.

Plan A, Plan B, Plan C were formed,
in case one failed, a new dream was born.

Relationships commenced, brief interludes end
whilst learning enough to make my path bend.

Suddenly someone enters my soul,
enhancing and supporting my strength and control.

Each experience is new, our lives now melded together—
fortified strength achieved to strive for greater endeavors.

Stagnation, always a state of mind foreign to me,
we continued to evolve—through additions to our family tree.

Priorities change as these lives are born,
challenges new—we were not warned.

United we tackled each day as a team,
continuing to believe our lives were a dream.

But one cannot survive the monumental strife,
of suddenly losing the love of your life.

The task of moving forward is all so new,
I became the one to hold it together with glue.

These are the ups and downs of life,
soldiering on through inner pain that cuts like a knife.

To replenish when spent,
I look into the faces of the children I bore,
enabling me to summon strength
to continue on once more.

WHY WOULD I BE INFATUATED WITH YOU?

Our first date seemed
destined to be,
two lives intersecting
so magically.

Conversation flowed,
subtle looks exchanged,
electricity sizzling, sparking sensations
within every gaze.

You said one day when married,
we'd reflect upon this night,
internally, I questioned your sanity,
but my curiosity beckoned greater insight.

Hours flew by,
we were out past three,
apparent to each,
we shared true chemistry.

Next day receiving your call,
for in different states, we lived apart,
absolutely serendipitous
that this relationship did start.

Within a few months, you moved to New York,
so together we'd be,
occasionally you mentioned this—
to be destiny.

When you next spoke of marriage,
by now, I was not surprised,
for it was clear that our emotional investment
had become synchronized.

Six years older than I,
you chose to ask:
If I was infatuated with you,
could this love last?

I quickly responded,
asking why this would be,
you were far from perfect—your true self
already revealed in its entirety.

Far from perfect was I as well,
perfection did not exist as far as I could tell.

You looked so shocked at my swift reply,
then our glances locked, eye to eye—
both recognizing that trust was cemented in full.

DEEP IN MY HEART

The tingle I felt whenever you were near,
the whiff of cologne when whispering in my ear.
The glow that radiated on your handsome face,
the magic felt when in your embrace.

Total trust between us shared,
never a doubt how much each of us cared.

Any story begun by me,
you could always finish.
Two unique individuals choosing to meld together—
our bond never diminished.

Regardless of what obstacles
life threw our way,
a shield we were, each for the other,
keeping foreseeable danger at bay.

Sharing disappointments
halved their misery,
whatever the day brought,
at night your loving words lifted me.

But our formidable union
was severed far too soon,
a world full of medical mastery could not
cure the illness that culminated in doom.

Beloved, two decades later,
I'm loving you still.

I've been granted perspective to appreciate
the abundance that existed from the start;
forever keeping the essence of you
secured in my heart.

TOMORROW IS NOT PROMISED

Recalling, my love, our wedding day,
pulling you aside into a private room, to say,

"Let's take a moment to realize
right here, right now
this moment in time,
our hearts, effervescent."

Indicative of how I've lived my life,
relishing joy when gifted,
for, inevitably, there will be strife.

Our tomorrows are not promised,
as we were to discover,
your life, cut short too swiftly—
I've still not recovered.

After so many years united as one,
our connection had burned into my veins,
your sudden absence from this world
did, indeed, drive me insane.

Replaying again and again a playlist
of melodies to which we reveled,
reliving those times, the pain reemerging,
I'm again—leveled.

Photo by Ashley Studio 1979

For I see you in every line I hear,
your green eyes shining with the love I held so dear.

My soul scarred forever from the pain of your loss,
it doesn't just scream, it echoes
within the monumental chasm that sorrow did cause.

This void can never be filled.

THE WARMTH OF HIS SMILE

When your whole world is turning upside down,
every hello that you utter is met with a frown.
Awakened with cramps, in so much pain,
had to travel for work, screaming kids on the plane—
drove me insane.

Upon arrival, asked for help with my bags—
not one person came.
The cretins I met with—
could not remember my name.
The flight home—
major turbulence,
seat belt warnings kept flashing.
Sitting next to me was some lady
who continuously yelled,
"We're crashing!"

Finally—get an Uber to agree
to drive to New York City,
the entire ride—the driver's jokes,
not at all witty.

Seems every tourist in the world
has come into town—
so many cars on the road,
mine cannot get around.

Photograph by DLG

I'd walk, but all sidewalks are crowded
with folks who seem dazed—
this entire day has left me
in an infernal haze.

When I get back, everyone's face seems so stern,
endless messages awaiting, countless calls to return.
Eventually the blessed time arrives
to make my way home—
frankly, I'm weary, right to the bone.

At last, comes the end
of this interminable day,
where the warmth of my love's smile
takes all the havoc away!

LOST IN THE FOG OF TOMORROW

And nothing was ever the same.

There was 'the before', then 'the after'.

A flawlessly cerulean sky brightened by sunlight.
The endless ringing of the telephone
that fateful Tuesday morn,
worldwide friends asking the whereabouts of my husband
as he was dressing to leave that dawn.

For any other day, he would have been there—
a blessed Angel above ensured his meetings
to be elsewhere.

Turning on the television to see absolute devastation,
panic had gripped—overcome our whole nation.

Tower One, now an inferno,
its gaping hole, afire,
suddenly, in plain view,
we watched, horrifically,
another plane flying directly into Tower Two!

Our phone continued ringing,
friends who feared that their spouses were there,
some had received calls indicating
their evacuation imminent,
en route, going elsewhere.

Too many—never to be seen again.

Any other day, he would have been there.

That fateful day, 9/11/2001, here in the U.S. of A.
the tragedy too immense—
too surreal to fathom in my head,
in just one company we would learn
more than 300 people were now dead.

More horror continued to unfold—
other commercial planes flying in our country,
now hijacked, under terrorist control!

The Pentagon, already under siege, devastation immense,
but the situation continued to become more intense!

Flames from a passenger plane
now incinerated, surging,
having crashed in rural Pennsylvania,
the television was now showing it exploding.

New York City, our former home,
suddenly unrecognizable to us,
massive crowds on foot, on streets, on bridges,
fleeing the 'City That Never Sleeps';
sirens screeching, police cars, countless fire trucks racing—
as an entire nation was weeping.

The world witnessed as each of the Twin Towers
proceeded to disintegrate,
a blinding thick fog descended,
color now removed,
becoming black and white,
the air, suddenly opaque.

Lost in the fog of a questionable tomorrow,
hearts forever ripped apart
in everlasting sorrow.

CASCADES OF PAIN RUPTURED THROUGH MY VEINS

Rapidograph Drawing with Faber-Castell Markers

Two independent personas joined as one,
intertwining through years together,
a formidable force in unison.

The promise of countless tomorrows
we expected to come true—
but you, my love,
were taken from this world far too soon.

Having watched an electrocardiograph
documenting your heart for weeks on end,
the moment arrived,—
a flatline, you no longer alive.
Sobbing now on my knees,
the recognition that I had failed—
could not make sure you survived.

Cascades of pain ruptured through my veins,
suddenly a young widow with two children
were all that remained.

The agony of unrest
almost pierced through my chest,
this was 'heartache',
actually consuming my soul—
my whole world,
now spinning out of control.

Shattered, suffocating, in air now too thin,
rational thought gone,
all proceeded to spin.
With desire and all sense of purpose, suddenly lost.
I did not dare to face the morrow,
our happiness, indeed, had a cost.

Babbling books
outlining absurdly defined
stages of grief—I soon learned,
do not nearly apply.

Indeed, there was to be no relief.

During all these years,
I've had no choice, but to endure,
for me, there still remains no cure,
without you by my side anymore.

DEEP AND DANGEROUS LIKE THE SEA

Destiny determined
the intersection of you and me,
both addicted to living on the edge,
intentionally bypassing tranquility.

Two dynamic, yet sensitive souls,
articulate and bright,
each capable of independently
torching their own light.

United in passion—
the mix made more divine.
You possessed an archive of life experiences, compiled,
so vastly different than mine.

We offered the other a new array of perspectives,
each had enjoyed living on the brink,
ignoring cautionary directives,
regardless of what others might think.

Combustible once joined,
emitting sizzling sparks of electricity discernibly,
satiated through years spent together,
each finding the other—
deep and dangerous like the sea.

Photograph by DLG

THE REALM
WHERE DREAMS ROAM FREE

Slinking down into silken sheets,
surreal slumber soon to surround,
it is here that mere mortal limits fail to exist,
a new wealth of fantasies, found.

Ambitious aspirations
are free to randomly roam
to captivating castles in the sky—
which can now appear to be home.

Those who were loved then lost,
can here be found—
accompanied by assorted angels
enchantingly flying around.

Vast visions ventured, fluently flow,
our unconscious can unveil
what, while awake,
we were unable to know.

Flights of fascinating fancy,
are here made to strikingly soar,
encumbrances that had hindered us,
now gone—herein, exist no more.

THE HANDS THAT LET ME GO

Came a time years ago
when my entire world caved in,
countless responsibilities assumed,
you, the Yang to my Yin.

Beloved, you were my rock, so solid,
whenever life seemed to overwhelm—
your calm perspective magically made
all approaching anxiety quell.

Those sunburned summer hands
that had held mine secure,
let go, the day you died.

I'm stranded now, lost, adrift,
amidst unrelenting tears,
hosts of memories remain,
but you are no longer here.

Absurdly wishing each moment
could be savored once more,
instead of that frightening, fiendish finality—
happiness coming to such an abrupt end.

If only I could place myself with you now,
within a protected hourglass of time,
to feel the warm embrace of your affection,
your arms again, encircling mine.

YOU SAILED AWAY FROM OUR EMPTY NEST

Eternally grateful to have shared
countless voyages with you on the sea,
traveling together across the ocean,
we navigated our vessel, the Lady D.

Cradled each evening by soothing waters
which peacefully rocked us to sleep,
delighting in our freedom felt
as we boldly ventured the ocean deep.

Our family eventually grew,
adding little deckhands birthed by me,
joining us, we motored onward,
this, what true happiness was meant to be.

Until our world caved in…

Too soon your soul was removed,
sailed away permanently,
you voyaged alone
into what became Eternity.

Our children and I left
within a glaring vacancy,
I—tasked to protect it on my own.

A searing pain remains on the edge
of what had once been our dream,
even full moonlight will forever fail to complete
that prior idyllic scene.

Continuing to search for you
through each ocean as it mirrors the sky,
you sailed away from our, now, empty nest
without the chance for a glance, or a loving goodbye.

THE LETTERS I WROTE

My world collapsed
the day that you fell—
you had recovered, returned to work,
all was well.

In an instant, you spiked a fever
of one hundred and four—
cried out, went pale,
then fell to the floor.

An induced coma deemed required
to deliver meds intravenously,
intended to reduce your fever expeditiously.

I swore I would bring you back home—
walking beside as they rolled you away,
removing you to commence an induced coma.
Hospital regulations refused me to stay.

Day and night
for weeks by your side—
leaving nothing to chance,
I, your lifelong bride.

No one could know what perceptions you heard;
omniscient doctors with differing degrees,
speculated with purported certainty—
that you retained every word.

The days, so long, the nights went on—
so much occurring in our family
while you were gone.

Deciding to put pen to paper
to detail each day,
you always said you loved
what I had to say.

Sitting beside you
I gazed at your face
as handsome as ever—
now fragile, with grace.

I talked to you,
internally praying, that you understood,
while penning pages a'plenty
with all the zest that I could.

The letters I wrote,
intended to be read together one day.
This dream crushed along with my heart
when you passed away.

A LONGING THAT DANCED LIKE A MOTH TO A FLAME

Within the sorrow of love, lost
I remain consumed,
that moment of reckoning—
air suddenly sucked out of the room.

Years spent together,
enjoying the adoration of a love, so sound,
then within one idle moment,
my beloved can no longer be found.

Years spent in unison,
remaining afloat,
the tides of life attempting
to rock our boat.

Total trust tendered,
no barriers, between,
our eyes, alone, could reveal ever more—
than mere words could mean.

Having jumped the broom
many years before,
blessed to relish that 'soulmate love'
so many yearn to explore.

But faced with
the unexpected death of your mate,
the foundation of existence crumbles,
to this—some will never relate.

Experiencing the depth of emotional pain,
so raw, impossible to hide,
my heart actually hurting—
tolerance of such suffocating sorrow,
I remained too distraught to abide.

Left lonely, with a longing that danced
like the light of a flickering flame,
the inability to face this monumental loss
became too much for me to sustain.

Wondering as my heart continues to ache
if a heartbeat can continue when pain is so great.
Is there a maximum degree of hurt
that this organ can take?

Remaining perplexed, if through eternity,
somehow, somewhere,
upon my entry into Heaven—
will I find you there?

FRACTURED REFLECTIONS

A fractured reflection
in the mirror before me,
the sanguine spirit of my soul
has lost its clarity.

A bursting heart
once abundant with joy,
has been pierced by sorrow—
left drained and hollow.

A life once painted
with vibrant hues
when well lit;
now left unstructured,
puzzle pieces that don't fit.

I know not who I am,
a mosaic of myself I've become,
a scattered remnant of a life
that has become undone.

Diane Lipton Gollub

ALONE I MUST WEEP

Alive long enough to know for sure,
when grief descends, there is no cure.
A line has been virtually drawn in the sand,
behind which only I will stand.

Those I thought I knew so well
have shattered my gift of trust,
its construct, a thin shell.

It seems that being there
when times are tough,
became too daunting a task,
for them—too rough.

A smile is all that they wanted to see,
not the now hollow illusion of this new me.

Realization that it is alone,
I have been left to weep—
such finality cuts through painfully,
akin to a knife plunged deep.

TRUE LOSS

Blasted, baffled, and bewildered, to learn
that the son of a dear friend
committed suicide.

Her harrowing pain and sorrow so deep,
absolutely overwhelming
her ability to speak.

She and I, friends for some forty-odd years,
each having lived through the loss of our husbands—
enduring unending tears.

But to lose a grown child,
father of four,
has completely left her undone,
for it cuts deeply into our matriarchal love
of our daughters and sons.

His sun sign appeared to be overflowing
with so much life,
but his moon sign
must have been filled
with intolerable darkness and strife.

My dear friend cannot process this pain,
her sorrow having silenced her voice—
mute, she remains.

I truly understand
that piercing pain of loss—sustained.
This ache—too deep
to give her a choice.

Each of our lives,
filled with times of bountiful joy—
but the lows seized all these gifts
with seeming intent to destroy.

I know not what to say
as I process this loss—
why must happiness always come
at such a cost?

INK AND SHADOWS

Lethargic and languid
I lie alone,
hollow and haunted—
the hulking spirits of those loved,
now gone.

Grieving with guilt for having wasted too much time,
too often, while they were alive.

Such a human failing—
to take for granted
those who are dear
while they are still here.

Presuming there will always be tomorrow,
or later...
to take time to tend to them.

Preoccupied with matters that,
in truth,
were so trivial,
I neglected to maximize those moments spent,
which I now know were so essential.

Left lost and longing,
I find myself immersed within ink and shadows.

THE POWER AND PULL OF TWO HEARTS THAT ARE FULL

If I could rekindle those embers of love,
splendid whilst sizzling,
then scattered above—
remnants of what some dream within fantasy.

The power and pull of two hearts that are full,
immersed within trust, for them—a must.

Memories morphed into mountains of smoldering ashes,
a compilation of stills appearing in distorted flashes.

If we could have remained at that moment,
when we first melded,
that time when, magically,
our two lives intersected.

If I could revive you, if you again were alive—
how much richer my life would have been
if you had survived.

CLOSING TIME

Free will does not grant admittance
into the Chamber of Sorrow,
wherein a one-way entry
suddenly descends upon one's soul.

The ticket is earned
once one's heart has been pierced,
searing pain has dissolved control.

Radiating within,
overwhelming one's spirit,
no amount of time shall ease its anguish—
enable it to diminish.

Forever after,
immersed within an unrelenting fog,
years can pass, but the hits keep coming;
now submerged therein,
deeper and deeper into an everlasting oblivion.

Numb, as happiness
has become a lost commodity.

Memories of a past are all that remain,
haunting each day,
destroying each night's slumber,
trembling—as we awaken to an Earth in decay.

A mirror reflects the reality
of time having gone by,
but no lightening of the burden,
as hard as we try.

There exists no closing time
within the Chamber of Sorrow.

I WISH I COULD HEAR VOICES

I wish I could hear the voices
of those who have been taken
far too soon.

Unending questions, unanswered,
silenced by the partition
between the temporary of now—
verses that which becomes eternal.

Regrets consume me—
too often was I dismissive whilst they lived,
foolishly, ignorantly,
believing we would have forever.

Now left drowning within the vacuum of loss,
yearning to know endless details
about the generations from which I emerged.

Unending questions, unanswered...

I wish I could again hear these voices.

Pastel

Nature & Earth

Beautiful Madness

Interwoven planes
of existence collide,
shifting perspectives,
daring to fling the obvious off to the side,
for it is within beautiful madness,
the artist resides.

Watercolor

The Spark Of Brilliance

If I were a straight arrow, I'd aim toward the stars
which make luminescent the heavens, and define who we are.
Prose and poems written for ages reflect insights,
appreciating the totality of nature's delights.

Sylvia Plath, e.e. cummings, T.S. Eliot, and Robert Frost
penned works portraying both joy and deep loss.
But Ralph Waldo Emerson's work, indeed touched my heart—
he wrote of the purity only nature imparts.
Emerson writes that men's eyes, splendidly illuminated by the Sun,
are a mere iota of light, seen by everyone.

The sun shines into the heart of a child,
an adult must contain this gift, not allow it—defiled.
The true lover of nature carries that spark as he grows,
preserving its brilliance, respecting its glow.

Emerson intentionally used the beauty within verbiage,
explicit, with great measure,
emphasizing that the harmony existing
between heaven and Earth, remains sacred treasure.

Ode To The Earth

Once the chill has gone,
rhapsodies of birds have begun to sing,
the dreariness of a grey winter
is now evolving into Spring.

The dewy mist casts a glow upon
red and white roses, protected by thorns—
the cerulean sky, a picturesque backdrop to the new dawn.

Multihued varieties of wildflowers
appear to be quenched,
regal red cardinals drink from sculpted birdbaths,
now drenched.

Bursting forth from the earth emerge rainbow colors, crystal clear,
perennials seem to know that it's their time to appear.
Chirping birds telling their tales of the night before,
indeed, nothing compares to the magnitude
of what nature has laid at our door.

The elegant shimmering coat of a delicate fawn,
viewed through the glistening cast of this April 'morn.
With pure abandon, she leaps forth with utter grace,
surrendering to the beauty of this time and place.

Pastel

I Immerse Myself Beneath Calm Waters

Tension, so pervasive,
its presence, palpable,
Earth at a breaking point
in terms of what is now salvageable.

Mental cretins on personal missions,
some clearly are insane,
slithering into positions of power,
from up high, they now tower,
so few intelligent leaders remain.

Ultra-conservatives have now been empowered,
seeking to drive into extinction
those refusing to cower.

For cookie-cutter replicas of themselves
are all they will abide.

Corporate entities currently infested,
run by those who are selfish, demented,
dismantling freedoms hard-earned,
judicial rulings, absurd,
struggling artists,
battling to remain represented.

Global warming deemed to be
an inconvenience, they see,
myopically their sole concern
is rearranging those comforts
they feel they have earned.

Wildfire contaminants,
casting orange auras upon inhabitants,
indeed, breeding disease,
HEPA filters installed for those possessing
adequate funds to continue to breathe.

I beg for relief
from disasters that abound,
immersing myself beneath calm waters,
where there is nary a sound.

We Are The Daisies

Generations of daisy kin have long told tales
of our age-old history of blooming on worldwide scales.

We are the 'Happy Flower',
eternal symbols of pure innocence,
but today we are struggling to survive
in a world that no longer makes sense.

In past, through the cycle of seasons,
we have consistently enjoyed,
come spring, popping up from ground,
our radiance, thus, boldly deployed—
continuously blooming until first frost,
end of fall,

however,

humanity has destroyed
what had been, a natural progression, stalled,
we now find there to be no true cycle existing at all!

Bursting and blooming
amidst an early onset of warm winter days,
then, overnight, suddenly doused beneath snow,
freezing, we begin drooping away!

Having always been equated as
symbols of new beginnings, we fret,
that herein lies our demise.

Once the seasonal glory of yesteryear,
we are now left to prematurely die.

Pastel

The Paradox Of Daffodils

Hardy survivors
of traumatically frigid winter seasons,
thus, daffodils emerge in April's breezes,
symbolizing hope for an array of reasons.

Their trumpet-shaped petals
announce independence and strength,
Narcissus bulbs can bloom perennially
for fifteen-year lengths!

Those that are white connote
purity, innocence, glee—
yellow ones yield signs of new beginnings
unveiled, for all to see.

But, be wary,
for appearance can surely deceive,
daffodils are not as harmless
as their stature would have you believe!

Sometimes, with just a touch
of their sap to your skin,
toxic harm caused from this irritant,
can cause an inflamed rash to begin!

Destiny Dreamed

Within the cosmos, circling throughout,
a universe of space, matter, and energy meandering about.
Planets, moons, asteroids all combust and combine,
dynamic forces catapult, soar forth, so divine!

Mere mortals are but microdots
amidst all this glory,
some presumptuous enough to believe themselves
capable of constructing their own allegory.

But the grand plan remains far too immense,
some get lost within,
or fail to comprehend 'til the end,
for it intensely continues, they cannot relate,
that we have only existed as fragments of fate.

Deceived to believe our import, unique,
striving to successfully convey
some semblance of mystique.

Cognizant too frequently that things happen
for reasons we don't understand,
we are mere particles within a spectrum,
each a prisoner of destiny, so grand.

The yearning to fathom our place
in the midst of this journey called life,
best be viewed with prudent curiosity,
imparting both joy and strife.

But leave no trace of tears
as each receives the gift to take part,
in the opportunity to create their own
unique works of art.

Aries Reborn

Succumbing to dreary doldrums
within the dark days of winter...
All wildlife appears to have vacated my woods,
what remains is the hiss of silence—

in which I do not hear a whimper.

The harsh chill of the season
has indeed, permeated my bones,
evolving into months spent within layers—
like moths cocooned in their homes.

I turn to Mother Nature,
yearning that she perform her magic,
ease my sorrow—
for with April's imminent arrival,
the sun will then be warmer, brighter, tomorrow.

Diane Lipton Gollub

Deer will resume prancing,
birds return to flight,
begin building their nests,
whilst singing songs of promised glory—
the essence of true delight.

As oceans come crashing
amidst nadirs and crests—its cascading waves
become lifted with a lightened levity,
frigidity warmed by sun's rays—within longer days.

'Tis glorious for me to reemerge from those layers
that had heretofore hidden my glee,
as springtime releases all Aries, reborn,
wherein, we are once again—free.

Dreaming Of Evergreens

With the approach of the winter solstice,
so imminent,
comes the opportunity to review
what, for us, is deemed relevant.

For amidst the daily demands
that descend indiscriminately,
chaos and confusion can conceal
what we most treasure, spiritually.

How pertinent becomes the promise to fortify
whilst dreaming of evergreens,
these symbols of timelessness,
their lush vitality pronounced—
vividly painting each winter scene.

Subdued within the somber stillness,
saturating Autumn's end,
becoming listless while witnessing leaves
of other trees descend.

There is fortitude to be found
in the proud sustenance of conifer trees.

Throughout time,
they have imparted the promise
of potential immortality.

I will dream of scenes of evergreens,
and feel restored, resurrected—
reflecting upon those memories
forever etched
in my heart, in my head.

Sea Breeze Wrapped In Sorrow

Decades done—alive long enough to learn,
everyone has a story to tell,
no one spared this rigorous roller coaster ride—
ascending to the highest highs,
then abruptly crashing into Hell.

Sauntering by the seashore
to be soothed by the symphony of the swells,
this soul is tired from
the torrent of tragedies having transpired...
I look to the ocean to again make me well.

Raggedly ravaged whilst caught in the riptides,
joyfulness, once in abundance,
has been rapidly extinguished—
then disintegrated.

Summers have always served as a respite
from the tediousness oft found in everyday living.
Now nearing August's end, too swiftly—
sea breeze has become wrapped in sorrow,
no longer the gift that keeps on giving.

Diane Lipton Gollub

Pastel

Utopian Garden

Submerged within a world of artifice,
I so often stumble,
frenetically grasping for some semblance of reality
as it seems to crumble.

Continuously transitioning interchangeable
personas in quest of success,
within a society that continues to be intolerant of discordance,
'tis imperative to feign happiness.

As such, multiple personalities are within my spectrum
to achieve maximum effect,
the audience never can be certain
who the real me is, yet.

A charade of masquerade vying
to produce an integration that is true,
occasionally donning a mask
that might not be appealing to you.

Whilst songbirds in slumber sigh,
I sink into Mermaid's Moon nearby,
this conflagration of varied facets
unveils a sojourn into the unknown,
to continue until such time
as I find comfort
in a skin,
uniquely my own.

Moss Woman

I now recline within moss, divine,
become one with the Earth
from which I was birthed.
My ear to the ground,
aware when strangers come 'round,
careful to shield, my head down,
immobile—for here, I am bound.
Occasionally found,
people's opinions resound;

'Have you ever seen
such a woman in green?'

I ignore what they say,
quietly calm, I do stay,
at peace once again
when they finally go away!

The Lost Gardens of Heligan
Photo by P. Carmen

All That Remains

Amidst chilly, foggy mornings,
my mind is continually rehashing—
finding myself standing
on deserted October beaches,
the robust roar of waves,
first swelling, then crashing.

So little to truly count on in life,
a reality, that oft seems, maniacal,
assurance can indeed be found within the four seasons,
their cycles still churning—
upon its axis, the Earth remains turning.

Each breath of mine emitting its shape,
visible in this brisk onslaught of autumn air.
Magnificent seagulls begin to descend,
seemingly appearing from everywhere—
they then tend to blend, as they descend,
into this seascape that appears to indeed, have no end.

Held captive within the sticky,
tangled cobwebs of my past,
so much that once made my heart whole,
never seems to last.

Cognizant that my ability to remember
signifies that I remain alive,
after ambling aimlessly
through days, into years,
straining to survive.

Recollecting that feeling, profound,
felt so long ago,
that with hard work,
there was nothing I could not achieve;
for youth gifts us with the promise
that concentrated effort can yield success—
this, I truly believed.

But life does tend to take its toll.

Approaching our waning time on Earth—
involuntarily, reflection commences.

We look back at our years with wanton wonder...

Amidst all that we've said and all that we've done,
what contribution has been made—
is it found in the fabric we've spun?

Grow With The Wildflowers

Arising with a heavy heart
to start this day,
world news blasting with horrific events
that have blown me away.

'Tis the sanctuary of an artist
to create an alternate space,
capable of making my heart whole
in a new time and place.

Wherever my heart takes me,
shall be a cathartic release,
using pastels to color in the emptiness
of blank paper as I please.

Inventing cotton candy clouds,
if that be my design,
whatever might be required
to regain serenity, peace of mind.

Within Spring's delight,
I choose to grow with the wildflowers.

Pastel and Pastel Pencil

Bleeding Willow

Thou hast become a symbol of strength,
of remarkable tenacity,
your drooping vines—
masking untold tales of so many visions seen.

There are those who remain afraid
they'll be driven insane
should you choose to reveal those tragedies—
that, before you, have been sustained.

Indeed, a tree of enchantment—
believed to align within cosmic Lunar cycles;
there exist those who claim the truth
to lie in a witch's domain—
those, who firmly believe you to be, somehow,
involved in sorcery.

Thy splendor, an integral entity, indeed,
the central essence of countless forests—
you stand proud,
resplendent with greens tinged in yellow and blue—
your confidence, both bountiful and loud.

Remaining steadfast,
possessing necessary fortitude to withstand
the mightiest of winds—
bouncing back from hazards, exposed,
such efforts, thwarted,
for you refuse to succumb
to any of these things.

As the somber sorrows of fall so eerily descend,
I beg thee to endow me with the knowledge you possess—
help me overcome the depression
that overwhelms me with sunlight's early end.

Left within incapacitating distress,
please share with me the secret of your success—
your deep-rooted stature, lushly as wide as you are tall,
in protest, you stand, protecting all you shield
beneath your rapture.

With unwavering generosity,
to all who seek shelter—they can rest assured,
you shall refuse to allow them to fall.

Powerful enough to withstand sap oozing from bacteria
which insect infestation brings—
Oh, Bleeding Willow,
tell me what fortifies you, unyielding,
to continue to overcome hardship's stings?

Kindly convey the sagacious perspective
that enables you to forever find the light.

As, for me, darkness begins to feel omnipresent,
days, too quickly shortening into night.

Hold My Hand A Little Longer

Yet again, another tragedy unfolds,
Mother Nature exploding as she furiously scolds.

Having gifted humankind
with the cosmic balance, she unfurled,
creating planet Earth using the care
with which an oyster unveils her pearl.

An intricately woven habitat
that humanity had been entrusted to secure,
however in their greedy rush to push boundaries, untoward—
people have dangerously shifted the natural order,
which took centuries to form.

Forever altering the environment
which we have been privileged to inhabit,
Nature's fury has been unleashed
throughout our beloved planet.

Wildfires rage, unending,
scorching all in their midst,
releasing foreign particles
which we now breathe to exist!

Mixed Media

An orange aura descends
upon all matter left in its wake,
destruction abounds
as the Earth continues to quake,
my hands remain extended
to lend aid to those who ache.

Springtime's Floral Breath

Wonderland lies before me, the greenest fields,
Springtime has unleashed the abundant beauty it yields.
An impressionist's palette, the lushest of hues,
pointillism-dotted landscape—a dreamscape come true.

The chirping of birds recounting their day,
bushy tails of rabbits, and squirrels, as they frolic away.
The sun casting illumination as its gift upon Earth,
Nature's blessings—my unending appreciation
for all that this is worth.

A spotted fawn snuggling beside a graceful doe,
vegetable gardens planted, their seedlings to grow.
An orchestrated masterpiece overwhelming in bounty and breadth,
transfixed, I feast as I inhale the aroma inherent—
within each floral breath.

Pastel

Rippling River

Into the melancholy midst of fields, I roam,
therein lies a rippling river,
that many a seagull call their home.
The whooshing of the water,
creating the whitest froth,
I cross it on a well-worn path
now covered with deep green moss.

Cattails spring forth,
from below rise their spikes—causing spots,
pointillism emerging, delicately painting the blue water
with vibrantly rich emerald dots.

Tall reeds stand proudly
upon these river banks,
choruses of birds compose
delightfully delicate melodic chants.

Blessed with a fertile imagination,
I envision others who perhaps ventured here
sometime in the past,
wondering about the lives they were living,
what memories had been made—
whether they still last.

An Unperturbed Lake

Tall tales forever told
of true tragedies, quaked,
happenings held hushed
within the periphery
of an unperturbed lake.

Couples, gone missing,
picnic lunches remain,
some who bathed in this water,
are said to have later, gone insane!

Once upon a time,
a home to fresh fish and snakes,
turtles, marsh birds, beavers,
their homes, in harmony, they made.

But solemnity has shrouded
this once lively place,
no otters, insects—
of fish, there's no trace!

What truth lies here, within this lake?

Though its appearance, remains quite serene—
here, no one dares venture,
it remains undisturbed—
like a fake fairytale scene,
wherein only silence is heard.

Beloved Of Autumn

The hissing of cicadas
fill the night with their symphonic score,
the sun has chosen to no longer rise
to the top of the sky anymore.

In the east, oppressive humidity
has now started to lift,
inklings of dry, cool breezes
have briskly begun to drift.

Green leaves suddenly in view,
swirling, whirling,
drifting to the ground;
squirrels stashing away acorns so slyly,
when they think no one's around.

Deer changing in color
from fawn to shades of grey,
their white tails remain fluffy,
as they prance away.

Some trees begin turning
those shades of yellow, orange, red,
the last of the perennials, now their time to bloom,
finally arising from my flower beds.

Most beloved within Fall
is that specific smell seeped in the air,
apples, spiced pumpkin scents—
the fragrance of autumnal perfume,
inhaled everywhere.

Pastel

Blue Ice

Pink and turquoise shards of ice
glisten with delight
crystalline structures appear to magically
scatter rays of pink and blue light.

Glaciers formed slowly,
compressed ice, if you will,
variations in pressure whilst forming,
yield refractions of light, resplendent,
amidst the crisp chill.

Symmetrical-shaped hexagon columns
randomly align,
radiating pink and blue optics,
refracted, they glisten—each unique in design.

Meteorites which, throughout time,
crashed on Earth sporadically,
their components oft discovered
within blue ice, periodically.

A rare sight to behold,
perhaps two and a half million years in the making,
it's strength a reminder—
to care for the planet we risk forsaking.

Footprints On Glaciers

Horizons, now misty
due to polluted air,
lungs breathing poison—
toxic fumes, everywhere.

Our oceans, once beautiful,
from sea to shining sea,
no longer provide a healthy domain—
with sea life in danger, they no longer live free.

The natural order of progression
has significantly changed,
as human ignorance insists
upon having nature rearranged.

Greenery leveled
to make way for grander homes,
diminishing wildlife's ability to flourish—
reduced to skin and bones.

Children holding buckets,
walking beaches, collecting shells—
now left to sort through
washed up plastic
amidst garbage that smells.

Footprints on glaciers have become visibly clear,
as warming temperatures deteriorate
our precious Earth's atmosphere.

Sitting In The Moon

For billions of years,
I've relished sitting in the Moon
viewing alien creatures attempting to land—
this, to me most inopportune.

Curious creatures appear sporadically,
attempting to pluck pieces from this place,
seemingly absurd that they bother—
so much else remains in Space!

They should be aware—
asteroids, comets, pieces of ice, and rocks
can be hurled in our direction—
its impact, a shock!

The latest are these strange Earthlings,
fallaciously believing themselves to be welcome...

Leave us alone!
You've ruined your home—
succeeding to pollute your once-pristine atmosphere
all on your own!

Quite comical, these spaceships
in which they do venture,
arriving in spacesuits and such,
uninvited, they enter.

In their selfish attempt to unveil
what has not yet been uncovered,
pieces then retained of the Moon's unique treasure—
they proceed to discover.

I take this in with a well-earned perspective,
see their desperation unfolding...

For while they feign introspection,
interest in all they are holding,
and though Nature has for some time
been furiously scolding...

their ignorance and greed has caused them to leave
their own planet Earth—decomposing.

Stardust Parade

Who would believe that wherever we are,
we are united with nature on Earth—
all bodies composed of the residue of stars?

Meteoric dust
from irresolvable nebulas, made,
after falling to Earth
in a Stardust Parade!

Saturating then, into living things—
our bodies, the vegetation we eat;
becoming the nutrition which
makes our bodies complete.

Whether delving within
to portray the inner depth of our souls,
or gathering inspiration
to artistically express all the beauty we behold,

an eternal cycle fortified, thereby completed,
through poetry woven with shimmering stardust.

Befallen Dusk

A caliginous atmosphere descends within the befallen dusk,
that which was familiar, can too readily become obscure.

Instinct, shifting us to recollected memory—to trust,
into a stygian sky, we find ourselves suddenly submerged.

Within somber melancholy, sinking into an abstraction,
its vagueness—absurd.

As it becomes decidedly difficult to discern
what once seemed tangible,
from what is now—frightful folly,
familiar sounds become distorted,
exponentially increased is the timbre of their orchestration.

Proceeding to test the core of
our inner resolve,
whether we be formed with fortitude,
or quickly crumble,
to then,
completely
dissolve...

The Monarch Butterfly

Be still my heart,
when the rare Monarch Butterfly is suddenly in sight.
'Tis said to carry the soul of a loved one, deceased,
delivering crucial messages which they bring to light.

Revealing it's time for transformation,
new direction, an alternate path to be ventured in life—
positivity offered to induce one to reroute
to a place removed from thus-far endured strife.

Their habitat has become
severely threatened,
due to climate change, worldwide,
essential milkweed required to ensure their survival
has now been limited due to pesticides.

With reddish-orange wings,
daintily dotted in white,
these splendid creatures shine lustrous—
iridescent and bright.

Believed to be a sacred gift
to observe one flying in sight;
a revered treasure, a vision—divine, indeed—
sourced from a Supreme spirit
to those deemed in need.

THE FACETS
OF A NATION

EARLY TIMES OF SWEET YOUTH

Once upon a time
there was a *childhood*,
a veritable delight,
safe to play kickball in the streets,
imaginations, free to take flight.

Staring up into the moving imagery of clouds
while lying on crisply cut lawns—
first-time crushes, giggling friends,
laughing together, sleepovers 'til dawn.

But laxly regulated toxins, negligently released
into our country, once pristine,
now poisoning humanity—
disintegrating what has now become
the antiquated American Dream.

The call to contain further calamity
cannot occur swiftly enough,
the preservation of early times of sweet youth
has just become too tough.

The beauty of our land which reigned supreme,
now relegated to occasional references
in yellowing library books, it seems.

The vestiges of calliopes and carousels,
becoming ghostly mirages
within childhood memory—
with immense trepidation,
we struggle to navigate through
this hazy mist of unknown territory.

BACK WHEN I BELIEVED

When I was just a child, the poetess Emma Lazarus
became my inspiration one day in the library;
choosing to venture into my first adult-section autobiography,
I enthusiastically chose to tackle it,
armed with a substantial dictionary.

A woman of substance was unveiled to me,
learning that she had set the standard in the 1800s—
a lone woman fighting oppression, absent boundaries.

Emerson, Browning... so many renowned poets
lauded her in her day.
Thus, "The New Colossus"
was commissioned to be inscribed
on The Statue of Liberty;
a sublime message—it eloquently conveyed.

As a youngster, it inspired me to believe
in the potential to change the world, for the better.
It seems our planet has forever been replete with monumental turmoil,
bringing too many, unneeded displeasure.

Decades later, my perspective has radically shifted,
once a hopeful youngster, I had sincerely believed
my diligent efforts could help someone's sorrow be lifted—
I had the power to see it achieved.

However, society has changed,
morality—now rearranged.
We are today, viewing illegality run rampant,
with no consequence for such deeds—apparent.

Our planet has become
so steeped in disaster,
society has lost its sense of joy, hope—
essential laughter.

Tumult literally cascading
within actual tidal waves—
a total shift done to the balance of nature;
people spewing hatred, violence,
unfettered discrimination.

Is peace even possible?
Can anyone be saved?

'Tis a sad state of affairs—
when one born with the desire
to lend aid to those in need—when required,
armed with advanced degrees,
an elite education, attaining positions—aspired,
now comes to feel baffled, totally impotent,
as to how to even begin to reach those
who choose to remain ignorant.

OH, TO BE THE THUNDER

In all my years
never have I seen an America like this—
those elected, selected,
now reduced to arguing like kids.

Monumental is the magnitude
of what needs to be fixed,
however those empowered to do so,
continue to engage in juvenile antics.

Within The Supreme Court,
once revered, the true arbiter of right,
now sitting are those in lifelong positions—
already influenced by glittering lights.

Failing to recuse themselves,
as all lawyers must
when a potential conflict of interest exists,
to eliminate possible questions of trust.

Instead, we find them participating
in consequential decisions
which benefit their own friends and family,
decision final,
no revisions,
they are not even overseeing themselves!

Too many elected officials who took oaths
to represent Americans equally,
have chosen to do the least work possible,
most selfishly.

What is to be done when symbols of propriety
refuse to comport—
instead waste each day idly, collecting salaries
which our ever-increasing taxes support?

Hate and toxicity let loose in our land,
what hope exists for Americans in positions less grand?

A lightning bolt must be thrust
into this tornado that spins.

Oh, to be the thunder,
with the capacity to make it begin!

WHEN TEARS FALL LIKE COSMIC DUST

Throughout history,
though wars have always existed when forged,
we were taught to continuously hope
for intelligent compromise to be reached,
possible once an agreement was formed.

At one time we lived in a nation
which chose—once united,
to solidify against those atrocities,
decidedly uninvited.

However, we are currently immersed
in too much turmoil within.
With no consensus of identifiable solutions being proffered,
remediation of strife in our land has failed to begin.

Anxiety has grown climactic,
hatred abounds amidst massive frustration, discontent.
How did America, which held so much promise,
lose sight of what Hope actually meant?

When fears fall like cosmic dust,
no relief available, nor found,
what can humankind do to maintain its sanity
amidst the wealth of hatred that abounds?

Diane Lipton Gollub

THE TIGHTROPE WALKER

That precarious balance
forever is tested,
a tightrope walk between
good and evil, manifested.

Enticements throughout life
will always dangle,
choices to be made continuously,
deeds can readily entangle.

Cognizant, our time on Earth
will be gone in the blink of an eye,
this massive burden of worry—carried,
as to where we will be after we die.

Holy Bibles all replete with chastisements,
should one not lead a life that is kind,
eluding the grasp of evil each day,
requires great strength of will and mind.

Alas, the Day of Reckoning shall come to pass,
for we know not when all grains of sand
will trickle
through
that
Grand
Hourglass.

LOVE IS THE RELIGION

So much turmoil
for countless years,
battles fought—innocent souls slain,
families shattered—shedding tears.

The human need
to feel we belong,
has yielded unnecessary hatred
with roots that are strong.

Virtually all with intellect
can concur and agree,
there exists a power greater
than our own family tree.

Many born into a trusted culture,
oft branded as religions,
an Almighty power is appointed, given a name—
though varied and distinct,
its essence, the same.

Love is the religion
when examining its core,
once understood
peace can prevail, be restored.

LIFEBLOOD

Through the tumultuous seas,
our vessel violently veering through waves,
'tis the lifeblood of fishermen
to bear weather so grave.

Within the perilous pitch of our seafaring ship,
we cast our lines into great depths—
nets extended in length, never certain, our bounty,
what, if anything, we shall get.

Heaving and swaying,
we are willing while praying—
prisoners of vast oceans,
our pursuit remains steadfast.

For abandoning our quest,
to us, an unknown notion,
as the life of a fisherman requires
unflinching and unending devotion.

Together, we're kin, from anglers formed,
reliant on the unity found and bound within mates.

We sink our lifeblood into sailing these seas,
praying to safely return, unharmed
to those who anxiously await—
our true-blood families in homes that are warm.

RBG

Nothing uttered or written
can possibly express
the true significance of losing
Justice Ruth Bader Ginsberg.

Whilst our nation is floundering in distress,
justice struggling to survive access—
we yearn for her contribution
to progressive growth in our nation
to be, somehow,
revived.

This petite, fair, formidable woman,
ahead of her time,
fighting for equality, impartially,
making injustice a crime.

RBG had a mind that creative geniuses possess,
no argument too insurmountable
for her to assess.

Few words need be spoken,
pondering, constantly in gear,
possessing the ability to fathom perspectives
others preferred not to hear.

Diane Lipton Gollub

With foresight to grasp repercussions
of interwoven decisions,
standing passionately as many tried
to alter revisions.

Strength of character, grace,
diligence and strict morality,
enabled her to process
complex issues in totality.

Her research continued
throughout the night,
tirelessly assessing what was wrong,
fighting for what was right.

So many mistreated throughout history,
already feeling the pain,
of losing this woman of substance—
forever remembering her name.

WOMEN GIVE LIFE, NOW DEMAND FREEDOM!

Enough is enough,
as we unite with pride,
no longer will we allow ourselves
to be cast aside!

You peons who seek to diminish
us dismissively,
however, do you think you entered
this world initially?

We created you,
you arrogant, ignorant, pathetic souls,
now you dare to belittle us, seek to debase us,
place us within your control?

It is women who gave you the lives
that you abuse with such ease,
seeking to eliminate our freedoms,
which you have wrongfully seized!

A force with which to be reckoned,
we women of heart and mind,
we will not kowtow to the likes of you,
or anyone who is unkind!

Many of us remain victims
of varied abuses, worldwide,
mental, emotional, or physical—
this, we shall no longer abide!

Beware of the might,
before you, represented,
encapsulated with grandeur, when we stand as one—
insist that our rights be protected.

Declaring we will not concede—
we shall not be undone
until justice is restored
to everyone!

THE PUPPET MASTER

He presumed the world
to be his stage,
it was his imagination that created
each script performed, writing each page.

The Maestro accepted no flaws,
nothing short of perfection,
mistakes would cause a performance to halt.

Intertwining of strings—
failure to bring puppets to life,
unfathomable, unpardonable,
sourcing to him—undue strife.

Consequences, harsh, would then be unleashed,
it would necessitate the destruction
of all guilty parties—
their existence would cease.

Wood smiths endlessly laboring
to carve works of art,
artisans meticulously painting features—
to tell them apart.

Each production need be appreciated
by an audience of one,
for he was the sole arbiter
determining the future of all participants,
narcissistically dubbing himself—
The Puppet Master.

Diane Lipton Gollub

IT'S TRUE WHAT THEY SAY

It's true what they say, it never changes,
history repeating itself throughout the ages.

Though this is the nation where liberty
resoundingly became the chant of the free,
those who have towered
over those who now cower,
shall not grant them
the right to do harm to me.

Endless tides have come to be filled,
but they remain insufficient to contain
all the tears that have spilled,
released by those who have either lost their lives
or their will.

THE UN-CREATOR

What characteristics
lie deep in the soul
of a peon of a person,
in need of wielding control.

Perchance a spineless spirit,
lacking confidence within,
one whose ego was squashed as a child—
a true sin.

What coping mechanism
might then be employed,
their intent turns to attempting—
to rob others of joy.

Often evolving into bullies,
spreading unfathomable evil,
relishing in smothering any joy that they see—
in hopes of reducing others to their miserable level.

Choosing to surround themselves
with those whose frailties can be assessed,
to better aim their jabs—
inflict the most harm—as they could care less.

These are the 'Un-Creators',
intent on dismantling whatever pleasantry they see,
absent their own confidence,
they will not allow happiness to be.

Twisting reality, telling lies with no cause,
these Disciples of the Devil
lack the conscience
that gives healthy people pause.

But, be patient, for their lack of character
will come to the fore,
karma is truly a bitch—
watch what's in store!

For there soon will be no audience
for their stories to tell,
indeed no postcards are available
in their destiny—Hell.

OPEN AIR PRISON

One need not be physically incarcerated
to, indeed, be constrained—
for in the land of liberty,
breathing free no longer remains.

Kindergarten politics have shattered
the hardest-earned human rights,
fifty years of legal progress
have been vanquished with perceptible might.

A nation in which those residing in open-air prisons,
this presently—the truest insanity,
for a preponderance of ignorance
has become our nation's majority.

LIFE GOES ON

The wheels of the bus go round and round
all through the town.

Too afraid to board the bus?
Too insane to ride the train?
Victim of crime in a city?
What a pity!

Crime is up, nothing's done,
in free fall—no safety net to land upon,
guns or knives, who's to see
if the next victim is you or me?

BUT

when the victim is a child,
the NRA suddenly goes wild,
let's blame the one who shot the gun,
which could be purchased legally by anyone.

Only an idiot can fail to see,
that they're available to anyone for a mere fee.
Hence, the reason they must be regulated,
so that their omnipresence can be abated;
for prisons do not contain the hate,
overcrowded—felons expeditiously
are released from their gates.

Recidivism is a cycle as old as time,
patterns unbroken,
repeated offenses,
new crimes!

Politicians pander to their public
to get elected.

Life goes on.

SIX YEAR OLD LEFT TO PLAY WITH A SMITH & WESSON

In Indiana, a young man,
leaving his apartment for the day,
saw a small child in a diaper alone in the hallway.
He was waving a gun, every which way,
closing the door quickly—
he told his family to back away!

His mother came to see for herself
what could be up.
Upon opening the door a crack,
carefully peeking out,
this child pointed the gun at her face,
said with a smile,
"Look what I got!"

'911', immediately called, police responded,
awakened the father who denied owning a gun,
after a cursory search—they left,
for in 'open view', there was not one.

The diligent neighbor proceeded
to follow—flagging them down.
Showing police the video she had taken
of the little boy waving the gun around.

The cops had no choice but to return to the scene,
finally asking the little boy,
"Where's this gun,
do you know what we mean?"

The diapered boy pointed to a closed roll-top desk,
in which was found,
a fully loaded Smith & Wesson,
containing a lethal 15 rounds.

Dad now arrested,
the charge, 'Child Neglect'.

With such abysmal consequence,
how many disasters shall it take—
to get gun control implemented,
for everyone's sake—
in every one of the United States?

MENTAL HEALTH AWARENESS

Why are we not immediately addressing
the ongoing risk to the public at large—
when it's clear through mass shootings,
too many guns are wrongly discharged?

The fragility inherent in mental health,
too often, tossed to the side,
starting as youngsters, children must be taught
to be in touch with their feelings inside.

A society that seeks to reduce
heart disease, diabetes, and such—
encouraging children to incorporate
physical activity into their lifestyle so much.

One cannot drive a vehicle
without yearly maintenance done.
When will it be deemed essential—
recognizing the import of
Mental Health Awareness while young?

Another mass shooting done by a child,
the immediate presumption—
that parents ignored
a child who was 'wild'.

Those warning signs,
though perhaps evident, went unheeded,
the public's outrage was continuously blasted
across every media stage:

"Why was intervention not done,
as all victims are being placed into graves?"

That delicate dance done with a child as they grow,
as parents in the midst of chaotic days,
so busy earning a living—
what don't we know?

Are we, as parents, truly cognizant
of those things, our children don't tell us or show?

Statistics have shown an astonishing fact—recognized,
that mass shooters have been too often consumed
by thoughts of suicide—disguised.

Their underlying desire was
that they take their own life,
this—felt before deciding to lash out—
and shoot innocent victims, now sacrificed.

The numbers that accumulate
are indeed beyond daunting,
the ghosts of souls prematurely released—
remains haunting.

627 mass shootings in the U.S. of A. in 2023,
with more than 6,964 already dead in June of 2024,
averaging 43 per day,
AWAKEN
to this ongoing unnecessary tragedy!

This subject needs to become integrated
as part of raising a child at home, in school—
no longer deterred.

Society must deem it a priority
to address 'Mental Health Awareness'—
for it cannot be inferred.

CRUCIFIED HOPE
IN TURQUOISE WATERS

What keeps me up at night
is the immensity of the scope,
a citizen of a country
whose history prided itself on once offering hope.

My fellow Americans,
to those caught up in elementary school histrionics,
maliciously, selfishly, debasing each other,
you've been bewitched—presently catatonic.

With irrational arrogance
some purport with delight:
"Only I truly know what is wrong,
absolutely what is right!"

I have been alive long enough to see
societal patterns shifting in front of me.

What was clearly defined has now become obscure,
worldwide catastrophes cumulatively escalating.

I remain afraid—dreading what's in store.

Shining seas have been polluted
by those mistreating this gift
that Mother Nature bestowed.

The contamination of turquoise waters—
its consequence, increasing;
the significance veiled by those who remain
ignorant or disbelieving.

Crucified hope has become the order of the day,
absent certitude, that salvation is on its way.

The strain has proven too much to withstand,
Mother Nature's dissatisfaction, manifesting in ire—
seeking culprits in every land.

Perched in battle, Earthlings are destroying
each other in a deadly dance—
choosing to stubbornly maintain
a uselessly rigid, decaying stance.

The angels cry, as they woefully mourn—
doubting in unison that their descendants
will survive a new dawn.

THE ESSENCE OF A BULLY

There exist some people who remain vacant within,
never having acquired inner confidence.
In vain pursuits to muster some semblance of self,
they remain clueless—know not where to begin.

Many have lived their whole lives feigning pride they don't feel,
what strength they exude stems from nothing that's real.
The depths to which they sink to feel themselves rise,
is typically a result of debasing others—in everyone's eyes.

Slinging malice—aforethought, their weapon of choice,
bellowing loudly to drown out another's voice.
Hence the coping mechanism such a person learns to employ,
in their attempt to boost confidence, they rob others of joy.

Many claw their way to the top of a post,
select friends beside them—those who bullies like most.
Often masking ignorance, as they lack self-esteem,
their interpersonal relationships have always been ones that are mean.

Surrounding themselves by those who remain
deeply afraid to contradict the insane behavior—too often displayed.
Twisting reality, telling lies with no cause,
absent conscience that gives a healthy person pause.

Diane Lipton Gollub

Throughout history, cult leaders have been analyzed
to comprehend how so many get caught up in their lies.

Ultimately, their lack of character will come to the fore—
what does a bully have left?
As anxiety mounts, he sees walls closing in,
suddenly cognizant—facing the end of his quest.

Left treading water, praying his narrative will prevail,
he consistently creates distractions—watching idly as his enablers go to jail!

The danger of failing to contain the influence of those so unwell,
can escalate into the tragedies that our history now tells.

INTERVENTION

If in some way I could change just one life,
it would be a beginning.

The classroom filled with thunderous footsteps,
the shrill squeak of chairs pulled to and from desks,
setting the stage as my job began—
tackling the components of abuse within families.

The art of conveying legalese to ears, not attuned,
dissecting the subject matter into its forms,
physical, emotional, sexual—
to teens who had become numb to such atrocities.

Reaching out to them in an inclusive manner,
shaping circumstances into ones that were familiar.

Interest piqued, comments spring forth;
"My girlfriend's father bangs her every night, but she lets him."
I patiently clarify that perhaps telling him was the most she could do.
"Trapped in such smothering circumstance, she reached out to you."
Now making clear what he could do.

Outlining the anonymous reporting system
available to anyone—statewide,
sensitizing teens to indicators that their peers might exhibit
when trapped within the trauma they hide.

I am uplifted by seeing sudden sparks of revelation in some eyes,
they were not alone in their misery, from abuse endured—
perhaps they could emerge with some semblance of pride.

Next, chatter is heard when the bell rings,
as the next class enters.

RESURRECTION OF AMERICA

Negativity can be
found within a cluster
of unhappy souls
bound together with bluster.

Each alone lacks
sufficient strength to impart
the hateful chaos
they have chosen to start.

Humanity has been given intelligence
to enable thoughts to differ,
they need not blend together
nor be sifted through a filter.

Most tragic is when those wielding positions of power
lack the perspective required to enable
acceptance of innumerable ideologies,
other than the ones they bring to the table.

These clusters build
impenetrable walls,
preventing crucial progression
from being installed.

If the sum of this energy
was more positively directed,
for certain, the strength of America—
could be resurrected.

NO GRADES FOR KINDNESS

Children certainly
do learn what they live,
their measure of propriety,
relayed through examples
society gives.

'Twas a time when faith in higher powers
imbued some measure of integrity—
fear of repercussions in the afterlife
led most to tread delicately.

Generations passed on customs and values,
thereafter maintained by their progeny,
children reveling in tales told at bedtime,
the most warm allegories.

Until focus shifted—wherein academic success
became paramount within societies at large,
school districts competing
to produce higher rankings by far.

Squeezed within the parameters
of a twenty-four hour day,
children having lost the necessary
free time in which to play.

Those children who possess more sensitive souls,
often containing hearts of pure gold—
are steamrolled,
left by the wayside,
remaining out in the cold.

Some deemed too slow,
or worse, oppositional;
school districts condemn their acting out
by implementing their dismissal.

This, now compounding
the pressure they already feel—
that the perspectives they have
are not even real.

Thoughtfulness and empathy, too—
now diminished, suddenly swept to the side,
no longer deemed a priority
to generate or instill personal pride.

For no grades for kindness
are dispensed within academia,
societal shifts, sadly,
have induced heartless hysteria.

ANGELS AND DEMONS

And when the angels decided
to shake hands with the demons,
a meaningful measure
of morality collapsed.

Gone were the values
passed down through generations.
The North Star—
vanished.

The compass that had fostered the peace
existent between nations,
its magnet has now lost
its power of orientation.

Empathy disintegrates,
compassion dissolves,
kindness and generosity
no longer evolve.

The focus now has shifted to selfishness,
what can I do to make myself stand out—
demonstrate to colleges that
I'm beyond qualified, no doubt?

Apathy has commenced, reigning supreme.
Calamity abounding, conflict astounding—
derived from those souls, no longer concerned
with potential prospects of peace—resounding.

Chaos has indeed erupted,
for no boundaries of behavior appear to exist;
consequences for ill deeds done
seem to suddenly subsist.

Plans for the future
have become virtually irrelevant,
uncertain if the Earth
shall continue as a planet—permanent.

FREEDOM STRIPPED AWAY

What has happened to the law of our land
when political influence
places Supreme Court Justices
in lifelong positions, so grand?

"Lady Liberty" no longer wishes
to reside in the United States,
a gift to a nation now denying
its freedoms with haste.

'Give me your tired, your poor?'
Ill-equipped to help them anymore!
'Send those, the homeless, tempest-tossed to me?'
our Constitution promises all residence
in the land of the free!

Gone is morality
in most elected officials,
conflict of interests taints too many—
judicial.

The essence of insecurity
finds a home in closed minds,
dissecting which aspects of reality
support their own kind.

Their choice, to wear blinders,
ignore whatever facts contradict their scheme—
dismissing hundreds of years
of those constitutional interpretations
that American generations
dared to dream!

The 'Separation of Church and State',
written into our Constitution,
is being systematically eradicated.
The result, yielding unending upheaval—
Justices dismissing enlightened evolution,
relishing backward notions,
proposing solutions—medieval.

Shredding the multi-hued fabric of the nation
we, 'Baby Boomers', proudly wore;
shattering recognized rights relentlessly,
demonstrating, unyieldingly,
their lack of care anymore!

continued

Stripping women of their 'Right to Privacy',
merely the start of their demonic plan,
to rip apart the diversity
that exemplified America, once grand.

Continuing to berate all differences,
as expeditiously as they can!

Acid etching

INHUMANE
HUMANITY

COMBUSTIBLE

Daily doses of destruction abound,
Humanity defiantly, challenging one another,
whilst the earth spins around.

Segments of the populace,
remain insecure, pervasive in their plight,
harboring hatred against all, but clones of their kind—
the only ones they dare deem to be right.

Ignorantly, obliviously, absent perspective
of the grandiosity that Nature has bestowed,
people are arrogantly, selfishly, upsetting a balance
that humanity might not again know.

Amidst the cumulatively cascading chaos
which consumes our planet each day,
some are seeking fuel for fierce passion
to instill some semblance of security.

COMBUSTIBLE is the content of all weapons available—
destruction possible, at anyone's command.
The goal: to find solace in the promise of safely containing
those effervescent glowing embers—
potentially scalding their own hands.

Those in pursuit of goodness,
vow to extinguish the evil which serves to defile
any inkling of true happiness possible
wherever it may be found.

Staunchly, standing formidably steadfast,
united, in purpose so sound,
within the purist sanctity of commitment,
that was, within virtuosity, bound.

A FRAGILE NOTION

A fragile notion
born with delicate emotion—
battered, bruised, defeated,
donning protective insulation—
now alone...
Survival demanded
that I completely retreat
into a barrier zone.

A defense against
bulleted blasts of continued scorn,
propelled by heartless personages—
their words prick like thorns.

So careful now
to shield all emotions, thoughts—
to never again be subjected
to those caustic onslaughts.

Caught in webs meticulously replete
with overwhelmingly sticky deceit.

IF I COULD SAVE THE WORLD

With a magic wand—
I'd dispel notions of envy and greed;
alter the balance of fortunes
to provide each what they need—
banish from existence
those who cause misfortune to bear.
If I could save the world,
tranquility would reign everywhere.

TONIGHT, THE MOON SAW ME CRY

Tonight, the moon saw me cry,
asking, why was my heart unduly heavy tonight,
why so despondent,
what caused my plight?

I replied that I have, for some time,
been overcome with deep fear;
this world has become contaminated with hatred—
everyone shedding such tears.

Nations vying with nations,
sisters at war with their brothers,
people, everywhere, their frustration bursting—
in turn, have lost respect for each other.

Too many countries harboring hatred,
their citizens, unhappy themselves—
rational thought and justice have apparently
been filed away on shelves.

The moon then replied,
it too, was dismayed,
for people had greedily disrespected treasures
that the Earth had conveyed.

Neglecting. Misdirecting. Misspending—
all wonders that nature bestowed.

The moon bequeathed the rhythm of time,
the modulation of tides,
filled us with the notion of hope
that had once yielded personal pride.

Together, the moon and I mourned
what had been an Earth, so pristine—
once blue oceans, now plastic-laden—
humans forever failing to say what they mean.

The moon and I, our souls steeped in sorrow,
concurred, 'twas almost as if in a dream,
or so it did seem—
due to droughts, once-fertile pastures
are no longer green.

The path forward is uncertain,
an entire atmosphere has now become polluted—
it's as if our new view is obscured
through a veiled, opaque curtain.

Perhaps in its wisdom the moon
has the foresight to project what will be;
but I remain afraid of Earthlings
becoming engaged in mutiny—
their last resort from unresolved tragedy.

NIGHTMARES

The curative power of sleep
cannot be implied,
physically, emotionally,
yielding restoration,
otherwise denied.

Every day—so unnerving,
worldwide chaos and crises abound,
'tis a wonder that anyone, anymore,
can achieve slumber that's sound.

Each night anew,
as to what lies within the recesses
of our minds,
for unresolved issues are revealed
during the repose of nighttime, we find.

Iridescent,
pearlescent,
opalescent
dreams segue inexplicably,
one to another.

Rationality has lost its foundation
as each night's journey is uncovered.

Occasionally nightmares occur,
startling enough to rouse us from sleep,
herein are those mysteries secreted within our psyches,
for our own minds to keep.

THE GARDENS OF YOUR OWN REALITY

Welcome to the wasteland
that is now our world,
feeling lost in oblivion,
amidst the swell of the storms.

Those who choose to eschew
the smothering sorrow, so daunting,
will find themselves adrift in infinity,
forever haunting.

For it is incumbent for a survivor
to summon forth the fortitude
to immerse themselves into a reality,
with a fresh attitude.

Stand strong,
creatively harnessing your own light,
for there will be no passage to paradise
for those who fail to fight for what's right.

Inventively manifest
the world you wish to see.
Become the God or Goddess
in the gardens of your own reality.

HUMANITY, ON THE VERGE OF EXTINCTION

Our planet's populace—enormous.
Nature's gifts, now corrupted—
damaged and diminished,
negligence and greed
have transformed the quality of existence.

Humanity, on the verge of extinction.
Insufficient nutrition, healthcare,
lack of funds to exist.

The surging result of habitat loss,
wildlife losing space to thrive—
though construction of homes is ongoing.

The homeless are left wandering,
too many can no longer survive.

Overpopulation is inevitably depleting finite resources,
we are imminently destined
to be dead beings,
walking.

Diane Lipton Gollub

ECHOING IN SILENCE

A story born
of a heart of stone,
birth from tedium
of years spent alone.

Heartbreak, heaving
upon a skeleton of bone,
enervated, crying,
releasing frustrated moans,
echoing in silence.

UNRAVEL WITH THE WIND TO BE FREE

What a calamity
when those bound by blood,
falsely accuse another
of clandestine, diabolical schemes.
With reckless abandon and unabashed arrogance,
nightmares have replaced
what was a family of dreams.

Attempts to unravel this heinous tragedy
which descended,
yearning for the winds to waken them
from this injustice, upended,
relations now maliciously fantasizing with ferocity,
delusional diatribes hurled forth.

Betrayed and bereft
by those once believed beloved,
suddenly cast as an object of derision,
resulting in permanent heartbreak,
an unnecessary condition.

Victimized within the wreckage,
needlessly left thunderstruck,
a tumultuous tragedy
litigiously launched
by those blinded in quest
of a measly buck!

SYNTHETIC EMBRACE

Superficially skimming the surface of commitment,
incapable of offerings, meaningful or consistent,
sashaying from one encounter to another,
apathetic regarding frayed feelings left asunder.

Too narcissistic to conceive
that your pathetic pretense is perceived,
I am choosing to deflect your synthetic embrace,
this, the maximum effort you can achieve.

Living life as you do, your sole concern is you,
proven two-faced, leaving others debased,
you are a disgrace
to everything I value.

ABUSE

Domestic abuse, child abuse, abuse of any kind,
those who are suffering feel
that they have gone out of their minds.

Children who grow up in a house of despair,
see no alternative for themselves anywhere.

Made to feel small, stupid, and inept,
this is their little world, the only family they get.
Scarred by this hell, they need intervention,
societies have created legal processes for protection.

Mandated reporters are now, a legal requirement,
to report indications of potential harm.
Child abuse authorities, trained to investigate,
they are deemed to be, now, formally alarmed.

Yet,
how many cases are not thoroughly checked,
marked as 'Unfounded',
the child is returned to the same neglect.

Meanwhile the most fundamental relationships
that these damaged children form,
will serve to teach them that
a true family strays from the fictional norm.

Now these innocents have been abandoned,
left to fend on their own,
perhaps adapt coping mechanisms,
while remaining chilled to the bone.

The cycle of abuse thereby grows ever larger—expands,
seeping, creeping, into other lands.

We will ultimately see its appearance within
descendants of that family tree.

NO ONE HEARS HER SCREAMS

Blinded by the glare of moonbeams
above the horizon,
the solemnity of the evening
serves to eradicate any magical moments once enjoyed.

Though nestled within a home that seemed divine,
atrocities unleashed therein
eradicated any peace of mind.

Now curled within a fetal position,
broken bones, fractured feelings,
scarred beyond recognition.

A stark awareness consumes her thoughts,
this, no longer the marital domicile
to which she was initially brought.

Cut off from those who had nurtured her soul,
becoming a victim of a beast who was out of control.

Warm memories of a childhood
in which she flourished, now faded,
replaced by the devastating hell
within this marriage, now degraded.

Only left to pretend within her mind's eye,
a cocooned encasement in which she can now lie.

Helplessly hopeless,
as no one hears her screams,
defeated,
teetering on the verge,
prepared to be extinguished,
bleeding in the blue that has surged.

Blinded by the glare of moonbeams above the horizon,
the solemnity of the evening erasing its magical moments.

Huddled in a fetal position,

broken bones,

fractured feelings,

soulless,

scarred beyond recognition,

abandoned by those she believed to be cherished,

defeated,

prepared to be extinguished,

bleeding in blue.

VENGEANCE IS MINE

The pretense of a happy marriage,
an image of delight,
conveyed to all until your psychotic nature
went berserk one night.

After scheming and methodically planning
the means to become my groom,
I was young, naive, an innocent,
unaware that life could yield dire doom.

Fallacious flirtations,
feigned interest in my thoughts,
like a chameleon,
capable of changed personas
at any cost.

Unctuously ingratiating yourself to me
at every twist and turn,
masked as a fairytale prince,
slithering through our courtship, like a worm.

Once "I Dos" were uttered,
you then advanced your scheme,
removed me to an isolated domicile,
a lavish abode oft imagined within dreams.

Cut off from all I loved and treasured
throughout my young years,
punishing me brutally for violating your rules,
I collapsed in tears.

No longer able to endure your wrath,
a day arrived, finally, you were preoccupied,
I slid out of your prison
along your curated Disney-like garden path.

This indeed, became the straw
that broke the camel's back,
your fury exploded,
snapping my neck in a brutal attack.

You then proceeded to dispose of me in pieces,
DNA extinguished in flames, no trace evidence remained;
you relayed to authorities that I had left—
as I had gone insane.

But vengeance is to be mine, dearest.
Karma is a bitch, indeed.
One night as you deeply sleep,
you won't know where or when,
you shall access entry into Hell,
to there, you will descend—
this to be your destined end.

IF LOVE COULD KILL

A masterpiece of tragedy,
to be doomed in defeat,
selfishly senseless sensibilities,
a precursor to destructive consequence,
its inevitability complete.

An initial attraction of momentous magnitude
between two highly independent souls,
a sizzling hot kinetic connection,
crackling chaotically out of control.

Solo survivors of prior relationships—
broken, gone awry,
each so fiercely independent,
claiming purported intent to unite,
whilst still maintaining their freedom to fly.

Each dominated by their determination
to inevitably master the other,
accustomed to a tendency to absolutely, in totality,
commandeer the will of another.

Categorically crippled,
neither capable of comprehending
the concept of compromise,
their quarrels caustically contaminating
any semblance of sustainability,
as assessed by outside eyes.

Their propensity to continuously disagree,
to remain forever out of sync,
neither willing to extend the basic courtesy
of truly caring what the other thinks.

Hence, trails of turbulence tread
through their tedious and toxic link.
If love could kill, slayed these two would be,
with their inability to truly care for another,
no doubt lonely for eternity.

YOU CAN'T TAKE IT BACK

The destruction of a sensitive soul
can be a gradual one.
It can begin the first time
their world comes undone,

when innocent trust is initially placed
by them into another,
who then chooses to violate it,
the force of this blow like no other.

Causing them to question their judgment,
their worth, to the core,
would it be wrong to believe
someone could actually love them anymore?

Emotional scars left,
armor begins to form,
more damage sometimes suffered
as a result of peer ridicule and scorn.

A face that was once serene,
projecting optimism and glee,
now subdued, far more cautious
as to what they allow others to see.

Submerged in a well of obsidian gloom,
survival now a race,
suffering solitarily in sorrow,
enduring grief with grace.

Psychological damage compounded
each time feelings fray,
negotiating who to trust
each, and every day.

Society replete
with those who never heal,
residing in virtual fortresses,
their true nature, concealed.

To those guilty of inflicting these horrors,
you cannot take it back,
you have permanently disfigured the soul of another,
an unforgivably reprehensible act.

Some victims are lucky enough to evolve
from this trauma, this life of despicable doom,
eventually acquiring strength to reveal themselves
behind these weeping wounds.

BOHEMIAN RHAPSODY

Interwoven with elegance,
aching torment profound,
the emergence of Freddie Mercury
was herein to be found.

Born at a time when being gay,
almost a crime,
his inner torment birthed the creation
of music, divine.

Too many years he had lived,
his inner lust buried inside,
until he finally was able to
display it with overt pride.

Consumed with his yearning,
for a lifestyle others were spurning,
the time finally came
when he enjoyed happiness, deserving.

Performing with grandeur,
he indeed, burst from his shell,
audiences quickly captivated,
awed by his spell.

Once crowned as Queen, he and his team,
their talent combined,
'Bohemian Rhapsody' was born—
brilliance divine.

Poetry, music and prose,
operatic interludes breathed life into its story,
swirling, whirling,
Freddie, freely unleashed in all of his glory!

But a tragic end
came to this now beloved friend,
after his true essence had been displayed,
upon a worldwide stage,

a lethal illness felled this dreamer,
he ran out of time,
taken from us, too soon,
during his prime.

WEIRDO

In somber silence, I've become an observer,
enduring the luxury of levity that surrounds me.

Lockers slammed when the bell sounds,
boisterous boys bellow as they slink into class,
giggling girls, amidst whispers, take their seats,
hallways now silent as classes begin.

Trying so hard to focus,
but I am consumed,
the content of the hour escapes me,
for I remain immersed within gloom.

The bell sounds, laughter resumes,
each shuffling on within their selected cliques,
glances in my direction, to them, it's a game,
as I have been deemed to be an oddity,
'Weirdo',
has oft replaced my name.

Their superficial souls now immersed
in the construct of after-school plans.

Only I know what awaits me.
More of the same.
The same route I dread each, and every day,
returning me to the nightmare
from whence I came,
to the House of Horror that is my home.

Laden with anxiety,
dread permeates me to the core:
Why must I continue to live within this Hell anymore?

Never knowing
when the creak of my bedroom door will sound,
my body forced to succumb to violation,
again and again, no salvation found.

Too ashamed to disclose
this Evil which pretends to be my shelter,
the eternal weight of misery, masked,
has served to cripple me forever.

DACHAU

Against humanity violations perpetrated, the most horrific of crimes,
cruelty continues to be inflicted— consequential wars continually erupt.

For some, these are the first visible, within their lifetimes.
Cult bigotry, exalted, by those with no moral conscience,
adopting hatred against peoples, innocents become the respondents.

I can recall, vividly,
traveling along train tracks in Munich, Germany,
a teen, beside my mother, about to see
one of the many historical remnants
of the most heinous of human atrocities.

Entering Dachau Concentration Camp,
established in 1933,
a creation of Nazis to exterminate all people
they elected to no longer see.

Located in a former site of a munitions factory
a mere 10 miles outside the city,
trainloads of victims were herded, brutally torn from homes,
once lovingly shared with immediate family.

Upon prisoners, brutal punishments inflicted,
from free movement, they were restricted,
bullets shot into bodies haphazardly.

Experimental medical procedures
performed on those with no actual affliction,
human guinea pigs, they came to be,
untold pleasure derived from those
who imposed these heinous, barbaric actions.

Above the entry gate, in German,
a wrought iron sign scrolled,
Work Will Make You Free,
a slogan that families, now eradicated,
would never live long enough to see.

Barbed wire strung around
the circumference of this horror site,
prisoners herded in,
as cult mentality caused untold evil to be inflicted
with such forceful might.

We then went into buildings
housing racks upon racks of bunk beds,
several bodies forced to sleep on each,
mattresses—non-existent, in this place
where humanity had been breached.

continued

Other structures entered contained showers,
an intentional façade that their forcibly stripped bodies
would emerge, clean—but in fact,
poison gas poured out from the shower heads,
with the efficiency to kill many at once
with its deadly, toxic stream.

Lastly, we entered the crematoriums,
where the dead were stacked en masse to be burned,
the horror of this happening in history
brought tears to my eyes, our stomachs sickly churned.

What stands out to me, so vividly,
beyond all this exposed inhumanity, is the outstanding reality,
that all those villagers who lived immediately within the vicinity
whilst thousands upon thousands decomposed,
did nothing to put an end to these crimes against humanity.

Pretending that they did not know,
with the smell of death so pungent, never ending,
I'll ponder until I die,
how they could not stand in opposition—

I will forever wonder why.

SEEDS OF DOUBT

Seeds of doubt for potential peace
are all that remain,
under mountains of layered limbs,
the hush of death, herein contained.

It is here that, indeed,
masked madness does lie,
where atrocities of humanity were inflicted,
bodies butchered with knives—
the breath of life, forever snuffed.
Broken branches of family trees,
seared,
then blown into dust.

Evil arrived here with monumental power,
like an untamed tempest,
it proceeded to devour
countless victims who were first forced to cower—
some being sexually abused,
others violently savaged
in their final hours.

Sprinkles of stardust cannot ever revive,
those who were beaten, battered, beheaded
whilst still alive.

SEASONS OF THE SOUL

A November moon seems to have overtaken
the infinite space of the sky,
for within the pull of Winter,
the sun no longer smiles.

Even the stars appear to be sleepless,
as these seasons of the soul unravel,
their shimmering sparks,
invoke no prospect of levity in the dark.

Heartbeats have been silenced in war-torn lands,
within the whistling
of the trees, are heard
the echoing laments of sorrow.

Glittering stars,
observe ongoing horror, from afar,
given a birds-eye view
of the unleashing of wars.

Apathy and exhaustion,
the result of wasted words uttered
to those who choose to be too blind to see.

Government institutions worldwide,
their bookshelves now laden with jars
of broken promises,
for the layered lies of politicians
have created an impenetrable barrier
for reason and rationality to revive.

We, poets, still dare to dream,
but our pens have become numb,
our quills, now still,
from the callousness of human nature, unfolding.

At the heart of our grief,
we mourn the senseless loss of innocent lives
at the hands of those consumed
by irrational greed and evil.

PRAYERS FOR PEACE NEVER VIRTUALLY VANISH

There exists a universal language of pain, laid bare,
as we sail down the winding river of life.
Time teaches, there is not a thing to be gained
by perpetual endurance of sorrow.

Try as we may to burrow,
shield those layers of ourselves that remain exposed,
having suffered the loss of too many held dear,
an eternal struggle persists to remain composed.

Festering feelings of fury emerge,
fueled by our incapacity to prevent needless harm,
nations continue to battle nations,
senseless deaths result, as all refuse to disarm.

Many continue, their battle, resumed,
though singed and scarred from injuries sustained,
their ire forged from flame reignited, as they continue
to pursue the justice they have vowed to maintain.

Prayers for peace never virtually vanish,
those seeking accord, continue their plea,
in hopes that those opponents created
through irrational conflicts,
will concede the need
for all people
to be free.

FROM WHENCE STEMS HATRED HARBORED?

Shrouded within a mourning veil,
breathing in air that has decayed, gone stale,
victims of violence, too many to count,
splattered within war-torn rubble,
amassing to an ungodly amount,
layers of limbs left huddled.

Sirens blaring relentlessly,
bombs exploding—villages leveled
as far as the eyes can see.

Actively decomposing,
remnants remain from family trees,
such needless death of immense scope and breadth,
victims slain, due to loathing.

Whatever is the point of all this savagery?

From whence stems hatred harbored
so deeply within some souls,
that they can smile as their commission of murder
cascades out of control?

With a planned destruction so incredibly bold,
proudly enjoying the torment, inflicted,
those callous, selfish, unfeeling, so cold,
now absent, the humane within humanity,
left abandoned, contradicted.

MY FAMILY TREE

What can it mean when the powers that be
align to make one date
a quadruple celebration
in one family tree?

Parents celebrate their anniversary
on the day their daughter is born,
she becomes a brilliant beauty
from whom greatness will form.

Eventually to become the wife of a son,
he, too, a shining star in the eyes of everyone.
What are the chances that his own mother's birthdate
be on the exact day, years prior, to his lifetime mate?

Coincidence continues, as yet to discover,
a younger sister who falls in love with another.
He also born, a different year, the same date,
her own sister sharing the same birthday as her mate!

One family, believed blessed,
to gather each year,
the first of September,
celebrating this gift that was so dear.

But families get tangled, I was soon to discover,
after losing my grandparents, my father, my mother.
Wretched rivalries form, accusations haphazardly hurled—
over inheritances received,
my blood forever curdled.

What's sad is that no celebrations
with them any longer occur.
All now severed from my life,
due to unfounded allegations, that date—now a blur.

PULL ME PAST THE PAIN

A brand new version of The Red Sea has emerged,
created from accumulated bloodshed
In The Middle East,
its volume converged.

A vast basin,
filled with oozing wounds—countless tears,
inhumane humanity perpetrating genocide,
all innocents, left, abandoned in fear.

Rational thought has apparently vanished
across the globe,
each day monumental tragedies abound,
continuing to unfold.

Before I drown in this immense sea of red,
become one more body floating amongst those dead,
pull me past the pain that has seeped into society as a whole,
allow love to break through to salvage our souls.

Let peace emerge, to reign supreme,
allow ample air to exist for all to breathe.

May hatred and prejudice be banned as toxic disease.

THEIR PERNICIOUS JOURNEY

The depths of desecration
to which devils descend,
evil manifested by their disciples,
meandering mindlessly, malice evident,
upon their pernicious journey to ensure
the destruction of their rivals.

Sashaying amidst the melancholia
veiled within misty moonlight,
soldiering onward with strident steps,
forging forward formidably,
fearlessly consumed by
their fiendish fervor
and might.

A trail of flames follows, its smoke simmering,
the consequence results in scorching sections
of the fabric of society—
then haphazardly left.

While swirls seep from steamy surfaces,
their victims remain
tiptoeing tenuously upon tinged teak floors,
ambient embers left smoldering, silently seething.

For these initiators of doom,
the fiery furnace of Hell awaits.

EMPATHETIC DISTRESS

Collapsing beneath the quantity of calamities catapulted,
current events, progressively churn,
an apathetic aura abounds,
seeming to explain why compounding catastrophes
continuously resound.

Whining wildly that world leaders
cannot attain resolution,
whilst the perpetrators of atrocities continue,
unhampered,
apparently receiving absolution.

International news, riveting, replete,
with varied accusations of blame,
aimed at anyone, anywhere,
deemed to be suborning genocide,
as mounting deaths remain.

We watch entertainment news carrying on,
humanity appears incredulous,
as on momentous dates,
gifting glittering objects to mates,
in light of world events—
becomes absolutely ludicrous.

Categorically, it seems incongruous to even
converse about trivial matters with ease—
welcome to the emergence of empathetic distress,
the newest, surging, incurable disease.

That feeling of overwhelming futility, in that, individually,
we cannot impart change, allow peace to prevail—
forever mindful that the maximum we each can do to end tragedy,
will not result in anything that will even register
on a worldwide scale.

Though empathy enables us to feel the pain of another,
we remain frustratingly aware,
how ill-equipped we are in making change,
unable to aid those immersed in dire despair.

In an attempt at self-preservation
avoidance becomes second nature;
a form of adaptation—somehow distracting,
an empty use of this energy spent—
becoming our sole means of avoiding collapsing.

What remains is our feeble outreach of compassion
extended to those suffering pain,
our acknowledgment to another that their plight is heard—
as we try to not allow ourselves to be driven insane.

PEACE IS A PRIVILEGE FOR MINDS LIKE US

Chaotic calamity has gripped planet Earth,
nations of people discontented with their worth,
some living in dictatorial regimes—
elected officials never saying what they mean.

Within unending minefields of catastrophe exploding,
sanctimonious sinners seeking salvation,
their sole concern—
preventing their own souls from imploding.

Intentionally masking their agendas
in manufactured misconceptions,
dampening the dreams of their electorate,
left to meander through a maze of morbidity—
becoming utterly desperate.

The minority who refuse to succumb
to the current state of affairs
find themselves on the brink of brokenness—
perpetually purging their pain,
seeking any hint of hope on the horizon.

Peace will not be possible amongst such pervasive hatred.

It is left to the dreamers to lead the way into survival and revival.

Wisdom & Hope

The Shared Pen

Behold the efficacy of just one voice
capable of proposing alternatives for change.
Limitless perspectives awaiting discovery—revelation.

The might of a writer to parlay written words,
sourced into beneficial enlightenment,
visible to those open to discover
new avenues of entitlement.

Now envision the strength of the shared pen,
creative minds collaborating
towards yet unseen possibilities.

Promulgating discourse between cultures
that had been in opposition—
amongst people who had never before
found a common thread.

Herein lies the power of the written word.

Love Is Not An Illusion

To know him is to love him,
but true effort is involved;
to him, amour an illusion,
its bitter consequences—never resolved.

Radiating a perspective, forever dismal,
exuded in his manner, severely curt—
my sense is that at some time in his life
he had been deeply, hauntingly hurt.

Possessed of a saturnine aura
as he goes about each of his days;
I'm convinced that I gleaned within his glance,
unhappy past experience with romance—
hidden facets of complexity
remain in his gaze.

Foundations of trust, ultimately secured,
I succeeded in peeling back those layers
that he had kept so obscured.

But the reward, so divine,
to watch the sudden thrill in his eye—
learning love is not an illusion, nor is it a lie,
but something to be savored—
humbly cherished until we die.

The Poetry Weaver

To greet the cycle of life anew
with the promise of creation—
blessed with an inventive imagination,
enough to ease the onset of futile frustration.

Capable of assessing situations
which seem hopelessly dismal to some—
perceiving rays of light that shine
through bleakly oppressive, opaque glum.

Repurposing hosts of givens
which have left others engulfed in sorrow—
rearranging the significance,
to offer possibilities of hope for their tomorrows.

I weave poetry into indigo night skies,
an artisan of magical manifestations—
retriever of what has been cast off as refuse
to those with lesser imaginations.

Utilizing creativity
to formulate new artistic visions therein,
possessing fresh fortitude,
unafraid to delve deeply within—I begin.

Oh, to be blessed
to possess a poet's heart,
capable of finding contentment
within a world now falling apart.

Diane Lipton Gollub

Sands Of Time

If all the beaches of the entire world
were to meld into one,
undersea life—radiant
beneath the splendid sun.
Each grain of sand,
representing
just
one
moment
here on Earth.
Sands of time can
become our true key
to what each life is actually worth.

Savor The Taste Of Humbleness

Compassion is key to achieving sympathy—
being mindful that each person's perspective differs radically.
There is no walk of life in which this does not apply—
perceiving the point of view of another
can only happen when you try.

Governing principles
within the course of criminal trials
is the standard of 'Reasonable Doubt'—
the assessment a person makes in such circumstances,
which is a reasonable one.

Mitigators ask each party to dispassionately see
what the other party involved
believes to be their reality.

When surfing the crest of a wave,
glowing, riding high, doing well—
remember that sinking feeling felt
whilst submerged within that trough—
once you fell.

For no one escapes the highs and lows of life;
happiness is often first appreciated
as a welcome relief subsequent to strife.

Never gloat, should earned success come your way—
for too many others are suffering
through horrendous days.

Savor the taste of humbleness when relieved of your sorrows—
be mindful that too many watching
are now struggling to make it through to tomorrow.

The Soloist

Arising with a heavy heart to start this day,
world news unendingly blasting
with horrific events that have blown me away.

Waves of sadness cascade as they crash over me,
for this is no longer the world
that housed the childhood
which I yearn to see.

The quest for solace
is so desired by the sensitive soul;
for fragile minds like ours...

In our attempt to reduce the anxiety felt
within a world escalating out of control—
we are too often frustrated,
as freedom has become—
methodically disempowered.

'Tis the sanctuary of an artist
to create an alternate space,
often a soloist, in this time and place.

Their retreat from the chaos—defined.

Wherever my dreams take me,
shall become a cathartic release—
whether it be words woven
to unravel the pain,
or music played on my piano
to help me feel sane...

Perchance, this day, I shall choose pastels;
for within the use of hues of color
I shall create my own vision of ease.

Serenity secured within my design,
whatever might be required—
that eternal struggle with which an artist is tasked
to instill their own peace of mind.

Kudos To
"Good Will Hunting"

A film I have watched again and again,
the first ever written, acted, produced—
by Matt and Ben.

'Good Will Hunting',
filmed in Cambridge, my college haunt,
pulsing with academia, blues clubs, debutantes;
forever reminding us of the genius Robin Williams possessed,
until tragic illness led to his untimely death.

Portraying so richly the angst,
the suffering Will had to endure—
emotionally scarred from childhood trauma,
while possessing such brilliance—he was not cured.

● ● ●

- The lifelong toll that domestic abuse does bring.

- The failure of courts to proactively—do anything.

- The beauty to be found within honest friendships—so true.

- The eternal dichotomy illustrated profoundly—
  questioning what should be deemed of value.

- The wrenchingly seizing sorrow felt—
  when soulmates do die.

- The ultimate release portrayed so sensitively—
  that freedom found when men can cry.

- The delicacy with which trust is earned—
  the benefits to be found within therapy, are told.

A masterpiece created by best friends with such care,
precisely produced and presented to audiences everywhere.

Release Me

I concede, indeed, to no longer request
to be taken back in time—
to when you were alive.

Now accepting that this be forever—
lost peace of mind.

I'm destined to carry you in my heart;
there you are indelibly settled—
we shall not be apart.

Though I cannot claim to be thrilled
by the meandering melancholy instilled;
the weather that Winter has brought—
leaving me chilled.

For I'm a true Aries—
awaiting the herald of birdsongs
that return in Spring;
yearning for blossoms to bloom,
rebirthed in breadth—
hope springing forth
from within Earth's slumbering depths.

Melting ice indeed reveals—
indelible scars from wounds that have not healed.

I pray that those echoes of emptiness
heretofore—quickly depart;
allow with the advent of Spring—
may sunshine's caress thaw my frozen heart.

For fierce whisking winds remain
sounding to a thunderous beat—
these distant howls resound
with Winter's reluctant retreat.

May those robins, wrens, blackbirds
who serenade lingering sadness away—
release me from profound sorrow
that has kept inner happiness at bay.

Pastel and Pastel Pencil

What Sound Is Heard At The End Of Time?

Time, a necessary notion,
invented by mere mortals—
attempting to apply some concrete definition
to the Universe's unending portals.

An abstraction created to somehow,
grasp the infinity of 'what is',
the imposition of segmented fractals of structure—
attempting to alleviate inner helplessness.

Some choose to turn to religion
espousing those theories that various Bibles relate;
trumpets sounding, seven in total—
allegedly, there will never be eight.

But, again, religion is yet another notion;
a source of hope created by Humanity
amidst their never-ending quest to apply
some defined sense of purpose
to obliviate—nothingness.

What sound will be heard at the end of time?

I hereby submit, most humbly—
for me, when time essentially can no longer be,
its tone, cadence, rhythm, or actual melody,
will, indeed,
become irrelevant to me.

Appreciation Gained Through Thoughtfulness

Listen up, little one, as I tell you the tale,
of those who misbehave,
and end up in jail.

We are inhabitants within one garden,
from seedlings we sprouted and grew,
please appreciate
that all wisdom I've acquired,
shall be imparted to you.

For here we coexist in unity,
and all adapt and adjust,
each respectful of the rights of others,
extending the courtesy of mindfulness.

We reside in close proximity
to others not of our kind,
we all must bend
and try to tend
to the needs of all those we live beside.

Forever be humble and grateful
for whatever happiness
you shall be privileged to possess;
before flashing it before others
who are in need—
spread generosity and kindness.

For appreciation is gained
through accord maintained,
intentionally extended
through thoughtfulness.

Embrace The Glorious Mess That Is You

'Tis human nature to be fallible,
perfection, indeed—an ideal,
only those with inflated egos
are eternally convinced—
that their projected personas are real.

Affirmation of self occurs
when one's limitations are accepted.
No one is infallible—one cannot always succeed;
we all experience the failure felt upon rejection—
humbling, indeed.

One can merely move forward,
summon renewed passion to strive to achieve;
and aim for that which we deem of value—
attempting to attain goals in which we believe.

No doubt, insurmountable challenges will arise—
come to the fore—ones that we can't overcome.
Defeat—deeply debilitating within our core,
becoming disastrous to some.

Therein exist the ups and downs
that comprise the journey with which we've been graced.
We've all traversed those roads leading nowhere—
through memory, these errors are painfully revived and retraced.

Embrace the glorious mess that is you,
as worthiness will be found within your essence—true.

Petals Of Change

It lies at the moment we emerge;
an odyssey comprised
of all we observe.

Chronicles of change are before us,
wherein we yearn
for rays of sunshine to come into focus,
wisdom to be learned.

Remain hopeful that faith can be found,
passion can stir,
in those imminent tomorrows
that are about to occur.

Individuals possess the fortitude
to transform what they see,
instill joy that is lacking,
create a new reality.

The power of creativity can indeed be derived
from those fireworks
which initially spark in our heads—
then come alive.

Therein lies the fuel
to weave a tapestry of golden memories,
woven with silken threads.

Aquatint

Focus your dreams.
What's worthwhile does take time for creation.
Success is no accident—
but is the fruit of sheer dedication.

Strive to comprehend those benefits
to be found within patience.
Realize there is no serenity experienced
while remaining complacent.

Petals of change are bound to unfurl
once given nutrients needed to nourish.

Life, an unpredictable adventure enjoyed,
each gifted their own seeds to flourish.

This Moment In Time

Foundations formed from perceptions discerned,
building blocks—a view of the world we each learn.
For within a Cosmos, its magnitude—vast,
humanity yearns for a structure that lasts—
as the Earth still does turn.

Within the instability we experience whilst drifting aimlessly—
we shall forever remain unfulfilled;
lest we choose to set tangible goals to move forward,
best utilizing our individual skills.

The pursuit of some semblance of security,
though perhaps is patently perplexing—
the alternative of remaining lost within uncertainty,
shall soon become far too vexing.

We proceed to construct an individualized reality
upon which to build a solid future—in totality.

Nothing ever remains stagnant,
within a world that is continuously shifting—
grab hold of a dream,
commence to construct a scheme,
or risk again, finding yourself drifting.

Noting that existence remains ever-fleeting,
what appears to be there, can tomorrow be gone,
realizing nothing will last forever—
make the most of this moment in time.

Fractured Promises

Do you know, have you not heard—
that there is a sacred meaning to be found
within the wonder of words?

Categorically conceived,
dictionaries written, printed, and bound,
to specify with exactitude,
that the definitions of words are entirely sound.

Perhaps your rearing was somehow—incomplete,
did you not ever learn?
That, within the foundation of one's morality,
a *proper* person is *always* taught—
integrity must be earned!

Combining those words uttered,
along with the speaker's intent—
is the only means for another to perceive
that what you said is what you meant!

For trust is now placed by the listener,
the belief now resides within you;
its fragility—delicate, easily broken,
if what you said is discovered, untrue.

For fractured promises, unlike bones,
will never fully mend—
alas, those possessing strong character
now have learned to not rely on you, again.

Symphony Of Sorrow

Composing with words—a musical score,
reaching deeply within my creative core.

The dynamics evolve
as words are passionately penned...
ever reverberating from inception—
to the cadence scored in the end.

Soothing Legato introduces the write,
as a chipper allegro transitions delight.

An angelic interlude, once a cappella is heard—
no music is needed to accompany each word.

Crescendo chimes in, gives rise to the heart,
yielding this symphony of sorrow, which I try to impart.

Raising a slight semitone,
introducing a sharp,
emphasizing emotion,
coming straight from my heart!

Betwixt and between varying harmonic phrases,
that are dispersed here or there—
emotions continually ascending,
within an orchestration, so rare.

Allowing a little levity to be interspersed—
with an arpeggio for texture,
bringing us to the final composed concerto—
culminating with a magnificent gesture!

Music, indeed, provides
sustenance to my soul—
bringing me clarity when life tends to spin—
completely out of control.

Art's Eternal Embrace

Centuries of artists
have endured countless woes,
the price of the sensitive existence
which burdens our souls.

Emotions plus intelligence
make a dangerous mix,
endless theories are expounded upon
to enable conflicts to be fixed.

For me, the choice is always
the path that has not been tread,
the road that has not been traveled
is the one I choose instead.

For infinite possibilities,
unconventional perceptions,
are yet to be revealed—
for inner passion blended with conviction,
birth a fortitude that will not yield.

If everyone's reality is individual, unique,
not like mine,
why rely on parameters that others
arbitrarily design?

Art's eternal embrace exists
by shifting those creative alternatives—yet to surface,
summoning forth instinct—
introducing a yet, unrevealed purpose.

The artist's mind riots
against notions already accepted.
The vitality that defines life
lies in discovering the unexpected.

How You Lose Her

Look to her
to complete your hollowness—
don't invest time in self-reflection
to remedy your infinite emptiness.

Beware if she were to befriend another—
a more scintillating lover
she perhaps will discover.

Thrust upon her
your own desperate insecurity,
attempt to selfishly contain
her resplendent, captivating glory.

Clip her wings
so she is forced to remain at your side;
diminish her value—corrupt the purity of her pride;
irrelevant to you that she's become unhappy inside.

Now you've done all you need to subdue her—

foolish man!

This is exactly how you lose her!

When A Dream Is Born In You

Each person is blessed
with unique qualities, at birth,
initially lacking perspective
to comprehend their innate worth.

Never diminish
the impact pending,
of those gifted contributions
that only you are capable of extending.

For it is a certainty
that when a dream is born in you,
your own fantasy can be woven,
come to fruition—become true.

Trust yourself
to sing your own song,
paint your own masterpiece—
don't play along.

For the integral ingredients,
belong to you to nourish—alone,
tucked within the imagination
you are gifted to hone.

The Scent Of Paper

Amidst the whirl and swirl of virtual reality,
are attempts made to impart information—instantaneously.

We become unaware of our surroundings as we saunter,
Bluetooth in our ears, our eyes affixed to mini-screens as we wander.

Obliviously ignoring those homeless souls,
whose sole abode is now in the streets;
streaming tears, their faces soaked,
seeking refuge under garbage bags—cloaked.

Our personal information has been dispensed,
stored in some cloud somewhere out in space,
knowledge is sourced from various media outlets—
someplace.

Libraries have been relegated
as historic relics from bygone days;
Kindle versions of books—
now replacing bound versions
of poems, novels, and plays.

But, I remain romanced by the scent of paper
which only print books can provide.
When unwrapping a book,
since childhood, enjoyed—
I am still extraordinarily thrilled
upon inhaling that fragrant aroma—
of the fresh ink and paper inside!

Let Go Of Fears

Stagnation is the root of futility,
voiding existence, until encountering death;
life must be lived to the fullest—
allow adventure to pull us—
until drawing our last breath.

A struggle to maintain balance
while we tenuously surf tides of change,
what appears to be destined today—
will likely be rearranged.

Upon a crest, we shall flourish—
only to then crash down into riptides, rough.
The inevitability of *gravity*
has pulled us into a bottomless trough.

'Tis the manner with which we face obstacles—
integrity, pride, truth, and morality
that can potentially become the very tools that steer us
through eventually encountered calamity.

It is the complete compilation
of the content of exploration,
which makes each person's life so unique—
gifting us the ability to climb mountains
that had once, perhaps, seemed too steep.

Let go of fears that paralyze,
each movement—too critically analyzed;
for this perspective remains too bleak.

If you believe, you'll achieve,
with power—conceived,
for no one is destined to remain weak.

How Much Can One Heart Hold?

Oft described in stories penned or told,
attempts to guess how much one heart can hold.

A mere ten to twelve ounces is its weight,
yet, worlds are unveiled with the key to its gate.
So much can be squeezed within this confined space,
magically making room, storing all in its place.

Beating hearts rhythmically transporting the blood of life,
absorbing all pulsating pain that is felt from incurred strife.
Heaviness, so palpable, while experiencing grief—
yet, the heart can become a safe harbor
when there's no other means of relief.

Containing immense joy—
this vessel can hold floods of happiness, once deployed.
If prudence and luck allowed to enter,
peaceful bliss can find a home at its center.

Caged In Your Regrets

Forever slumped within the somber sorrow
of suffered sadness—as if you were Atlas;
burdened with the weight of the world—
it's heft, driving you to madness.

A prisoner of the past
you have decreed yourself to become—
endlessly reliving those moments
in which you believed that you disappointed someone—
having misconceived that you failed to achieve.

Caged in your regrets,
you are your greatest hindrance
to experiencing that joy found in flying free;
thus preventing you, dear friend,
from fulfilling your enormous promise—
becoming all that you deserve to be.

My wish for you,
no simple feat for you to fathom—
is to release yourself from that useless guilt
which you erroneously conceived;
replace this wasted space with the purity to be found
within the passion you have now achieved!

One Hug Turns Every Tear Into Radiant Rays

Compassion—so simple to dispense
to those suffering dire despair,
as melancholia can consume all the light,
leaving one immersed in total darkness—so unfair.

Secluded alone within sorrow,
having mysteriously vanished from sight,
'no news' presumed to be 'good news'—
sometimes an incorrect assessment of another's actual plight.

If someone you know has not been heard from—reach out!

Let them know that their absence has not gone unnoticed,
of this—you are more than aware.
For one hug can turn every tear into radiant rays,
quench someone's fear, lift someone's soul—
their burdens now become eased once they are shared.

Dare To Care

step out on a limb
let the healing begin

make all our tomorrows
ones without sorrow

never too late
to stop all the hate

make sure all the hungry are fed
empathetically mourn those now dead

use your eyes to truly see with remarkable clarity
all the goodness to be gained so easily

step out of your zone
give the homeless a home

may tears shed by every girl and boy
become solely the result of overwhelming joy

become aware
dare to care

Pinpoints

We sensitive souls pen tales of our woes,
on occasion relating slices of life—
that nobody knows.

Be it within novels, lyrics, poetry, prose,
we are in search of catharsis—
from those tragedies told.

Indeed, we've created unique forms of art,
depicting our lives—
some, living in families now falling apart.

Once seemed so splendid, when they did start,
but quarrels, absurd rivalries—
ripped through their hearts.

Molehills became mountains,
while unhappiness continues festering—
increasing their magnitude to something unsettling.

Some consumed within such profound sorrow,
drained and isolated—
without hope for tomorrow.

Those lacking integrity,
attempting to enhance their mood,
treat unsuspecting innocents as though they are fools;
for in making others feel smaller—
they now envision themselves taller.

Each of us, a pinpoint existing within
a world that remains so vast;
it's a wonder if capacity even exists;
to find within one's lifetime—
true meaning that persists.

I Am Woman

The mantle has been passed
from one generation of formidable women
to the next—
enriched by kindness, integrity and wisdom,
maintaining the dignity
of the position they have earned.

Fleeting Facets

Forever aware that time won't stand still,
moments evolve into memories;
occasionally—some wretched,
others—remain ripe with their thrills.

Remember, when immersed within sorrow so deep—
the fright of the feeling that you cannot recover;
though smothering whilst submerged,
rest assured—its endurance is waning—
for soon, its threshold is over.

Awaken to possibilities that those next moments can bring,
our lives are composed of new wonders—unraveling.

There is no one who is free
of those fleeting facets that spin,
just when comfort is found, it can easily vanish—
hopefully unveiling fresh perspectives to delve in.

Selectively incorporate into your heart and your soul,
those aspects that serve to make your happiness whole.

May It Be Rainbows
That You See

Fireworks—currents of electricity marked by the setting sun,
a match made for eternity, serendipitous in design,
from two separate points in the Universe—
our stars intertwined.

Maturity had taught me
that time does not stand still—
relationships between anyone
require nurturing communication and skill.

Stagnation becomes the poison
which often bursts the sacred spell—
expecting your mate to remain unchanged
is offering life as a prisoner in a cell.

Not all possess the self-confidence required
to gift others their freedom to fly—
evolving, whilst partaking of richness offered,
as life so quickly passes by.

Never have I hidden that I am a sensitive spirit;
artistic and cerebral to the core—
thirsting to soak up perceptions,
for life is indeed a variety store.

If you think this is not the person you first met—
you misconstrued your view,
you decided to remain unchanged,
forsaking all that is new.

My darling, if this be your journey,
may it be rainbows that you see—
please recognize that it's you who has changed,
for this has always been me.

Fearlessly Allow
Your Facets To Shine

Beware the danger, inherent it lies,
when choosing to find happiness through another's eyes;
forsaking the many facets—those varying sides that are you;
allowing the facets of another to become
superimposed upon yours—that were true.

Become on your own someone of whom you are proud—
gift to those you love, the space for their songs to resound.

Don't lose who you are out of sheer desperation—
attempting to retain a union that was disjointed in the making.

And if you find yourself in the midst of a love that is real,
remember to proudly pursue your own growth—
this you need not ever conceal.

For as much as your beloved can serve
to make believe your heart is now whole;
time of death is an irrevocable finality—
that we have no power to control.

Take whatever time to emerge
from the catastrophic loss which you feel,
how individual is one's journey that commences
when we each try to heal.

But know, deep inside,
there exists in your core,
that person of substance
who you had respected before.

Beware of the danger,
as inherent it lies—
when you totally source happiness
through another's eyes.

Hope For A Brighter Tomorrow

Through a window to my past,
I find myself in a haunting
commenced by those ghosts
which lie in wait upon my shelves.

Somehow emerging from the confines
of carefully constructed photo albums
and frames displayed—
a virtual record therein of a life once lived.

Family and friends felt as strongly
as when they drew breath,
never was there the slightest forewarning
of their untimely death.

Suddenly abandoned and lost,
now that they have died—
I find myself on the wrong side of Paradise,
in that I, somehow, survived.

Oh, to sink into sweet oblivion,
if only those now gone, could be revived,
shelter me in that protective cocoon spun,
wherein I was once safely nestled—
not yet a widow or an orphan.

Left alone with my counsel—deflecting,
I attempt to avoid misdirection.
Thrust upon me from unfeeling persons,
pointed pricks from their needless aggression—
this malice shall not be recognized.

Delving into ink-stained imprints,
within my thoughts as penned—
I am forever in quest of components of clarity
to be extracted from confounding chaos, therein.

Struggling to not be consumed, overcome,
swallowed within solitude and sorrow—
this, my attempt made to avoid the extinguishment of hope,
within the prospect of the emergence
of those brighter tomorrows.

Those Wonders Unveiled In Spring

This shall be my fresh ode to Spring,
within the murmurs of March life renews once again;
hope found as I welcome those wildflowers—
already surging.

Luxuriating in the rhapsody woven whilst songbirds sing,
having become, during Winter, so tangled in evergreen;
seized to endure those challenges
that the frost doth bring.

Finding myself bewitched as new leaves begin to sprout,
Spring is evolving, there is now no doubt.

Bees begin buzzing, their quest to procure pollen has begun—
into honeycombed hope, their nutrition is spun;
then placed for containment within waxen compartmentalization—
to be ingested through the Fall.

The sun has agreed to again rise to the top of the sky,
its radiance filling my soul which Winter left dry.

Though there shall never again come a time
where we can again begin—
experiences, perceptions, emotions remain flickering,
none possessing a lifespan—lingering.

However fresh fortune can be found
whilst remaining spellbound
by the majesty
with which nature resounds.

Oil Pastel and Pastel Pencil

And If I Were To Die Today...

...and if I were to die today,
forgive me for how much has remain unsaid,
forgive all I have neglected to accomplish
while still breathing—getting distracted, instead.

If I were to die today,
pray, care for my children now that I'm gone,
please let them be aware
they always have each other to rely on.

Allow them to indeed
find the true happiness that they seek,
during this harrowing time of mourning,
bring them strength when they might feel weak.

If I were to die today,
please let my beloved friends know
that I have brought pieces of them with me
wherever I shall go.

If I neglected to indicate to them
fully while still living,
please share that their love and support
gave me the strength to go on—to continue giving.

If I were to die today,
please allow all to somehow share my words—penned,
for this is all that remains
as I've reached my life's end.

Within lie my perspectives,
my continuing quest to achieve wisdom and to learn—
to gain further insight into this world
as it continues to turn.

About The Author

Diane Lipton Gollub

Diane Lipton Gollub is an attorney, artist, musician, poet, and philanthropist residing in New York. A graduate of Brandeis University in Waltham, Massachusetts, she earned Cum Laude Degrees in Sociology/Criminology and Fine Arts in 1977. She then went on to study at The School of Visual Arts in Manhattan, creating portfolios in Graphic Design, Advertising, and Package Design. She began her career as the Art Director for Sasson Jeans, Inc. in New York City in 1978, at 22.

After marriage in 1979, Diane commenced the study of law at St. John's University School of Law in New York. Upon passing the bar exam, she commenced her legal career at The Office of The District Attorney in Nassau County, New York. Her philanthropic activities include work at Island Harvest, a food rescue charity that supplies food throughout Long Island, New York, becoming the Vice President of Community Relations at Child Abuse Prevention Services in New York, where she voluntarily taught Child Abuse Law in high schools on Long Island, and to Mandated Reporters. Also serving on the Board of Directors of The Rosa Lee Young Childhood Center in Rockville Centre, New York. Chosen to be amongst those selected to review a study of all public schools in Rockville Centre, determining what funds were needed for their improvement.

The proud mother of Hayley Meredith Gollub and Ross Brandon Gollub, Diane was widowed in 2004, losing her beloved husband of 25 years. She became involved in Instagram in 2019 through her daughter's suggestion as a means to lift her perpetual sense of loss and the grief felt within widowhood. Her poetry evolved after being embraced by the loving community of artists within Instagram. She remains forever grateful to all who have inspired her to feel that her voice should be heard.

Pastel